DEDICATIONS

The first dedication of this book is to our Lord and Savior Jesus Christ. He has made life worth living and given us a future to look forward to. There is nothing in life that we cannot face when Jesus is by our side. And when we close these earthly eyes for the last time, the first Heavenly sight we shall see is His face. I thank Him for His promise of eternal life and for His sacrifice that he made to make it possible for us to live with Him forever.

Trust in the Lord with all thine heart; and lean not unto thine own understanding. In all thy ways acknowledge him, and he shall direct thy paths. ~Proverbs 3:5,6

I would also like to dedicate this book Heavenly Dreams in memory of my dear little friend, Keith LeRoi Booker, Jr. whose journey led him to Heaven a little over three years ago. I am looking forward to the day I will walk with him again, but on golden streets with our Lord.

Keith LeRoi Booker, Jr.

KEITH

Keith LeRoi Booker, Jr. lived a full life for his 8 years and 10 months that he had on this earth. Keith lived all His life for the Lord, knowing from an early age that he might be going to meet Jesus earlier than most. He was diagnosed with leukemia when he was two years old and he spent much time in the hospital during his life. He learned to love life and live it at its fullest. He never complained about his illness, but at one time in asking his mother about Jesus' sufferings he commented, "If Jesus suffered that much for me, then I can suffer for Him." That was just weeks before he left this earth and at a time that he knew it was soon. He knew to leave this life was not to die but to continue to live on with Jesus.

Many people befriended Keith, the church people from his church, The First Pentecostal Church of Murlin Heights, a fire station who gave him his own fire jacket with his name, and an animal shelter who gave him a kitten and videotaped it for the news. A basketball team "adopted " him and carried him on their shoulders at the end of a victorious televised game.

The family practiced family devotions. At times, Keith would preach. I heard him preach about his being God's little lamb. I was very honored to be considered many times as part of the family and loved Keith very deeply. Keith loved me too. I still consider his family like my family: his mother Regina (an illustrator of my books), his sisters Tayvona and Shannon and little brother Joshua.

The last full sentence that Keith spoke was "Good morning, Mom."

Written with love, *Pat Behnken*

HEAVENLY DREAMS
In Memory of Keith LeRoi Booker, Jr.
7/17/86-5/11/95

I sit at your side and watch you sleep,
Memories of the day flooding through my mind;
I think of how sweet you look when you're resting so deep,
With the look on your face so fine.

I wonder as I watch, what you're dreaming about,
Is it your cat Bogie or your Snuggles bear?
Or are you playing and chasing your little sister about?
With your look, it could be heaven fair.

Do you feel the angels as they watch over you?
Can you hear their sweet songs as you rest?
Can you feel the Lord's comforting hand upon you?
All the dreams that He gives are the best.

Time passes on from those restful sleeps
And new struggles your life has gone through,
But upon your life, the Lord's hand He keeps,
And His blessings for you have been true.

You've suffered so much, now it's time to rest,
Angels of the Lord are standing quietly nearby,
Awaiting the moment you'll be the Lord's guest
And for Heaven's "Good morning" with this earth's
 "good-bye."

As you step onto Heavenly streets of gold,
 Jesus gives you a pure robe, white as bone;
Your body fresh and new will never grow old,
And you'll sing praises forever at God' throne.

When I have been chosen to come to Heaven so
 sweet,
You'll tell me all the dreams God gave you,
And with joy together we'll walk golden streets,
And we'll see all our dreams have come true.

~*Patricia A. Behnken*

THE LIGHTHOUSE

The lighthouse shines our way
And points us to the cross,
When hearts are empty and longing,
Whenever we are lost.

The lighthouse stands so tall
And shines its light so bright;
It shines upon our darkest path
And drives away the night.

When rocks are dead ahead,
We can't see where they are,
When the danger looms before us
He guides us as a star.

The lighthouse is our Lord,
He guides us night and day;
He watches us through troubled times,
He shows to us the way.

He keeps us always safe,
He lifts us from despairs,
He stays with us to comfort us
And shows us that He cares.

So put your trust in Jesus,
Give Him your heart this day
And let Him become your lighthouse
To always shine the way.

~*Patricia A. Behnken*
July 27, 1998

LIFE'S PATHWAYS

Life is strange, we all agree–
this life we live down here,
A maze sometimes it seems to be,
leading here and there,
Sometimes it leads down pathways straight,
where the road is clear ahead.
Then suddenly it bends and winds around,
so we're blind to what's ahead;
Sometimes it leads to mountain tops,
so green and fresh and clean;
The sunlight beams upon our face
and glitters from within;
But then the path abruptly drops
to valleys way below,
Where only dark and dismal thoughts
are the only things we know;
The sky seems overcast above,
and angry storm clouds rise,
But when we look on far ahead,
we'll gaze into Thine eyes;

I will lift up mine eyes unto the hills from
whence comest my help...
~Psalm 121:1

Lord, Thy right hand I grasp
as Thou reachest out to me,
I let Thee guide me on ahead
through the deep and perilous sea;
You lift me up in courage strong,
well knowing when it's through,
I'll reach that mountain top again,
my eyes still set on You.

~*Patricia A. Bayless Behnken*
1973

THE WRITING OF LIFE'S PATHWAYS

There is a story behind the poem "Life's Pathways." It did not have a real name until my book was completed as far as typing and ready to send in for copyright, even though it was written 20 years prior to that time. It was that poem that made me name the book "Pathways Of My Journey."

In 1973 I was going through a lot of things, including a divorce. I had never written poetry as such prior to that time. My rhyming poetry, if I tried, would have been something like–
I have a dog
His name is Trix,
He can really
pick up sticks
 --or something to that effect!!!! I could not write poetry. I could write short true stories or little thoughts (which could be considered prose poetry today), but nothing that would really be classified (at least in the past) as "real" poetry.

I used to at that time sit down and write letters to Jesus when things were troubling me or I just wanted to think. So one evening I got into bed and began to write a letter to Jesus. I wrote a paragraph or two, writing to Him about life. Then I started:
   Life is strange, we all agree,
      this life we live down here...
   a maze sometimes it seems to be,
      leading here and there.
I had written 2 1/2 verses, then stopped and went back to the beginning of the letter to see what I had written already to gather my thoughts to write more.

When I got to the last part I had written, I exclaimed "My goodness, this is a poem!!!!!!!!" So I continued to write until I felt like saying "Amen."

The poem was written...it was my very first poem in my life (still my favorite of all), and very inspired by the Lord. So this was the beginning of the gift the Lord gave me and the beginning of my poetry ministry. I had thought about telling about this incident in my book, but didn't know if it was really appropriate at that time.

When I first realized I was going to finish my manuscript and publish a book I was told, "Now you will have to have a name for your book." Instantly, my mind went to the poem. (I had been calling the manuscript "My Journal.") Without even thinking the name was on my lips, "Pathways Of My Journey." I didn't change my mind or even consider another name for the book. The poem I had never titled. I wasn't comfortable with any name, nothing came to mind. I just called it "A Prayer Concerning Life." When "Pathways Of My Journey" was ready to finish for the printing, the title was instantly in my mind, and I said to myself, "This is the name and has always been the name...I just didn't know it." So I felt the Lord gave it and the Lord named it–"Life's Pathways." So this is probably why this poem is still my favorite.

~*Patricia A. Behnken*

THE RAINBOW

One night I had a dream:
There was a beautiful rainbow~
the prettiest I'd ever seen;
The colors so bright
were shining down through the sky;
It was so close,
it seemed I could touch;
I walked up closer
and reached out;
I walked into the rainbow~
Sunlit rays of color,
filtering down through the air
surrounded me with beauty,
as it beamed on me there;
I was standing in the rainbow,
as it reached across the sky
and arched downward
to envelope me in its beauty!

~*Patricia A. Behnken*
July, 1993

INTRODUCTION

Patricia A. Bayless Behnken is author/publisher of "Pathways Of My Journey," an inspirational and devotional autobiography. "Heavenly Dreams" is her second book published. When Patricia first decided to put together a book of poetry, she found a poetry site on the internet and started to read. She was so blessed with some of the writings that she decided to invite other poets to join in the project. "Heavenly Dreams" is a collection of poetry gathered from poets in various states (U.S.). Together these poets hope that their writings will uplift, encourage and bless all those who read them.

SPECIAL THANK YOU!

I wish to express a special thank you to all the poets for sending me their beautiful poetry and for their desire to uplift the Kingdom of God. I especially want to thank those of you who went that *extra* mile with me in offering help and suggestions for different parts of the book. God bless all of you my friends! You truly make me smile. ~*Patricia A. Behnken*

Illustration by Regina Moore

The rainbow is as God's glory,
The cross is where Jesus died,
He's the light, our joy, returning in clouds,
When He'll never again leave our side.

Scripture references for the poem:
Rainbow: Rev. 4:3; Cross: Hebrews 12:2; Light: John 8:12;
Joy: I Peter 1:8; Clouds & forever with the Lord: I Thes. 4:17.

TABLE OF CONTENTS

DEDICATION	3
KEITH	4
HEAVENLY DREAMS (poem)	5
THE LIGHTHOUSE (poem)	6
LIFE'S PATHWAYS (poem)	7
THE WRITING OF LIFE'S PATHWAYS	8
THE RAINBOW (poem)	10
INTRODUCTION	11
SPECIAL THANK-YOU	11
REGINA'S SKETCH	12
THOUGHTS OF A POET (two short poems)	14
CHAPTER ONE 　　Praise Worship And Thankfulness	15
CHAPTER TWO 　　Hope Comfort and Encouragement	55
CHAPTER THREE 　　Stop Think And Consider	97
CHAPTER FOUR 　　Guidance Direction Or Admonition	113
CHAPTER FIVE 　　Christian Attributes Responsibility	129
CHAPTER SIX 　　Families And Friendship	143
CHAPTER SEVEN 　　Heavenly Promises	179
ABOUT THE POETS	182
INDEX OF POETRY BY AUTHOR	187

THOUGHTS OF A POET

CARGO

Every poem has a cargo,
Every poem a transport;
Most important is the cargo,
No matter what's chosen to transport.

Every poet has *his* style,
A transport, *his* message to say;
It's not so much the style we choose
But rather the message we convey.

~Patricia A. Behnken
June 23, 1998

TO WRITE

To write is what I need to do
To express what I can't say,
To put on paper what's in my heart,
So to others I can relay.

It's hard for me to say out loud
The thoughts that run through my head;
Whenever I try, they come out together,
And no one really knows what I've said.

When I write my words, I must stop and
   think
And read what I've written in pencil,
And then I know I've said what I meant
And the words that I've written are sensible.

~Patricia A. Behnken
December 27, 1994

PRAISE

WORSHIP

✝

AND

THANKSGIVING

JOY IN THE JOURNEY

Lord, I am thankful you made me
to feel the pain of life -
the fevers, frets, fears,
laughter, dreams, tears.
Living with our daily struggles
Knowing - Oh what joy is this journey!
so simple so pure so precious to say
thank You for this time, this place.

~Jack Ellis

WITHIN HIS LIGHT

With celebration and glorious elegance
Help us enclose those private memories
Our emotions, our dreams, our pleas
Of love, of pain, with acceptance,
To be filled with wonder in our hearts each
   night
To live, seek, learn within His light.
May the spirit, the joy, the hope, and fullness
   of existence,
Be consumed totally within His guidance.

~Jack Ellis

PRAISE IN THE NIGHT

The darkness of night overwhelms my soul,
But deep within my spirit a praise
Comes surging forth from deep within,
And faith rises up, the fears to chase.

The melody bubbles forth over again,
And joyful thanksgiving unto God I bring,
Comforting peace blankets my soul,
With praises to Jesus from my heart I sing.

~*Patricia A. Behnken*
April, 1998

PRAISE IN THE NIGHT TOO!

As I read your poem.......much to my delight,
it brought to mind many a prayer I've prayed
 at night.
When there is only silence and no one is
 around,
it's then I speak my heart the best I've truly
 found;
It's then too... I stop to take the needed time
to spend in prayer with my Lord so very
 kind,
Not letting the hassle of this world get
 through
and praise the Lord for all He's done and that
 He will do;
So like you, I too, give praise in the night
To the ONLY ONE WHO CAN MAKE
ALL THINGS RIGHT.

~*Gary Jenkins*
The Servant

PRAISE THE LORD ANYHOW!

God who made the fragrant rose
Also made the skunk!
One was pleasant to the nose,
The other one just stunk!

God who made the April shower
Also made the raging storm;
One brings forth the fresh spring flower,
The other brings forth great alarm.

Yet all things that God hath given
Have their purpose on the earth;
When someday we get to Heaven,
We'll discover their great worth.

Trials, we think, may be a curse,
But do not fail to look up friend,
Things could really be much worse
And eternal hell could be our end.

For God does use the strangest things
To bend our hearts to worship Him;
And one great thing that this all brings
Is an eternal home in Heaven with Him.

So do not fail to praise the Lord,
Giving Him glory wherever you are;
Try to be pleasant, sowing no discord,
And each time you need Him, He'll not
  be far.

~*Patricia A. Behnken*

JUST SING A LITTLE SONG

What a crazy day this is!
Everything's gone wrong!
I know I've found a solution–
Just sing a little song.

Lift up your heart in joyfulness
To praise and honor Christ;
Then and only then you'll see
What's worst can turn out best.

If we give in to all hard things,
We may as well expect
To reap ourselves what our faith brings–
What we believe, we get!

So turn around the "hard-time" day,
Praise God though all goes wrong;
To fight the battle, here's the way,
Just sing a little song!

~Patricia A. Behnken

THE PRESENCE

*...my presence shall go with thee,
and I will give thee rest*
--Exodus 33:14

You're so special to me.
You cared about me;
You helped me
through various troubles and trials
that I had to face.
When I seemed so alone,
You took away the loneliness.
When all hope
seemed to vanish from sight,
You put peace
into my inner soul,
And when all was said and done
You stood there by my side
and was my friend,
Your voice was never really audible,
and I never really saw You,
but somehow
I always knew You were there.

Your presence
is a known fact to me,
that without You
I would be nothing,
Although I don't know when,
someday I will see you
and express to You in person
that your presence
is my reason for living
And on that day
I know
that I will live
with You
FOREVER.

~*Lisa Marie Sackett*

IN HIS HANDS

From my hands to God's hands
I will turn over every care,
With complete and perfect assurance
That my burdens He will bear.

For God will surely accomplish
All that His hands receive,
Every need He will supply
Each sorrow He will relieve.

The problems I cannot solve,
The answers I cannot find,
All I commit to the Lord
Trusting in Him to provide.

As I turn over each burden
Asking that His will be done,
I will thank Him for the trial
And the answer that will come.

For through each difficulty
My faith even stronger grows,
As God reveals His loving grace
And new blessings He bestows.

~*Doris Allen Davis*
1997

CARRY ME

Carry me Master, carry me
Through days both bad and good,
O'er hills and mountains, in valleys too,
For I know You said You would.

Carry me Master, carry me,
When it seems I can't go on,
I know You are there, with Your hand
   guiding me,
Ever gentle, ever strong.

Carry me Master, carry me,
When that final breath comes for me,
I know You'll be there, with arms
   outstretched
You've always been, and always will be.

Carry me Master, carry me,
I now can see Thy face,
Such a beautiful home, no more worries to
   know,
Just abiding in Thy grace.

Carry me Master, carry me
To Heaven to dwell with Thee,
Lift me up close to You, far away from this
   world,
And to Glory, where forever I'll be.

~Kristi A. Butler
1998

SITTING AT HIS FEET

There's a valley that I'm going through
and it's right where I should be.
I see a mountain far ahead
though it looks oh so steep.

But I've got joy right where I'm at
because God's right here with me.
Come and look a little closer,
I'm sitting at His feet.

Well the mountain that is up ahead
is closer now it seems,
I listened to what God told me
while sitting at His feet.

He said that He really did love me
and was doing many things;
mostly things that I could not see
but were giving me sweet peace.

Well I have come a long, long way,
all His promises I'll keep,
as the mountain's getting smaller
I'll be staying at His feet.

~*Lisa M. Sackett*

REAL TREASURE

At the end of all my days,
the Master looks at me and says:
"Lacked you anything at all?"
"Nothing, Lord, that I recall,
just your being and nothing more
yet, richer than I was before.
For everything I've needed here
you've provided, and stayed near.
So there is nothing that I need,
all my selfish wants recede.
It's you alone provide the day
and you alone my constant stay.
When my body's heaven bound,
there will be my treasure found.

~Richard L Elam

GARDEN OF THE HEART

When peace is nowhere to be found
and confusion and chaos are all around,
I withdraw to a place of sacred ground;
one that lives within my heart.

When winter strips the landscape bare,
I can close my eyes and at once I am there.
The sweet scent of lilacs fills the warm spring
   air
in the garden within my heart.

And as the world goes rushing by,
I can sit and watch the butterflies
dance across the turquoise sky
in the garden of my heart.

Planted with faith and nourished by prayer,
each peaceful pathway tended with care
Only hope and assurance await me there;
in the garden within my heart.

~Donna M. Givens

I KNOW I LOVE YOU

My soul wait thou only upon God;
for my expectation is from Him.
Psalms 62:5

When the enemy of my soul tries to smother
me out - with my past failures chasing me
about,
My heart's flame flickered and fought not to
doubt.

When I can't find the words to say
And I don't know just how to pray,
I know I love You...

When I feel I'm in bondage and can't get free
And my days are dark and I just can't see,
I know I love You...

When I'm fighting with all that is within me
And life's wheels just keep spinning and
spinning,

When my race in life feels there is no goal,
"The prize of the high calling" cries from my
soul;

Then in my mind a voice sprang anew:
"For your dreams and hopes are just in view.

Continue on serving the one in you, wait on
Him,
His love is true.

He knows the day when your trials will end
And your days of rest with Him will begin

Peace and comfort that He gives even now
Will fill Heaven's beauty all around.

He will give to you great joy from His love
So sweet, when you gently bow down and
   lay at His feet."

The voice in my mind spoke all to be said,
A reality check my soul had been fed.

My eyes filled with tears as I felt Him so
Near - A soft voice I heard said only,
   "My Dear."

In the Spirit so clear, I began to see
Jesus was looking down on me.

As I gazed in His eyes so pure and so true,
He softly spoke, "You'll make it through."

From the depths of my heart, with words
   so few
All I could say was...
"I know I love You."

                    ~Inez Regina Moore
                      March 12, 1997

THAT I MIGHT REST

Let me give my heart unto
the Master of my soul,
that I might come to rest inside
His arms and be made whole;
Let me pour my cares onto
the altar of His name,
so that I remember that is
why for me He came;
Let His gentle Spirit come
and take me far away,
so that I might rest in Him
and find strength in His way;
Let me give my life to Him
so He can lift me up,
and fill this wretched emptiness
with his ever flowing cup.
~*Suze Vanderbec* 8/28/97

RAIN ☼

Is rain the tears from God above
as He looks upon us all,
That cause the seas to swell and crest
as they begin to fall?
And is the wind of Angel's wings
as they soar above the skies?
You sense sometimes their presence close,
if you will only try;
Then this I hope must be the truth,
it makes good sense you see,
Sunshine is smiles from God's good will,
I believe that it must be;
For everything He is to me
while He watches from above,
You see I know I especially need,
first, foremost His love
~*Kelley Lundborg*

HIS GIFT

Lord please forgive me
for things I've said and done,
For wanting to cut my ties,
for wanting to run;
You had given me a special gift,
one I couldn't see;
I almost sent the gift away,
shattering all dreams;
All the love I'd ever want
was there before my eyes;
But I could not see it,
I thought it all was lies;
But then You touched my heart and soul,
You made me realize,
because You have such love for me,
that gift was my present life.

~*Tracy Tammaro*

HIS PRESENCE

Through the ages of ones life
there's happiness and despair;
Through all the times we couldn't hold on,
there was one who was always there.

Though we could not see Him,
nor touch His flowing hair,
Though we could not hear His voice,
somehow, He was there.

Only a presence could we feel,
though understood or not;
He always kept Himself so near,
He is the Son of God.

~*Tracy Tammaro*

RESURRECTION

Is resurrection real enough,
or is this metaphor for life?
Did you really overcome
death's grip?
Can I believe this myth
as real or must I doubt more?
Would your revival
lead to mine;
a restoration couched in joy;
a peace penetrating the wounded heart?
Do I perceive the truth
or just a lie?
My fear is strong today;
and faith is weak.
But, how I need
your resurrection truth this day;
and how I wish
that everything I hear, I know.
For there, in that bare tomb
lies hopes and dreams
of future bliss, or scattered bones of death.

The place is empty now.
No body found.
What have they done with you?
We need a shrine
but there is nothing here to see,
no artifacts or relics.
Should we still worship,
even though we are not sure
that this was your
place of death?
Perhaps, I'll look around,
a better place might
be close by
where we can
light our candles,
sing our tearful dirges,
and lament your passing.

But wait.
Is that your voice I hear?
Calling me to turn around?
How can I face
away from here?
Yet, that sure voice
still beckons me.
Is that you, Lord?
Is this real?
Have you indeed o'ercome
the death that haunts us all?
And, if you have,
does this mean, I can as well?
Are there no bones,
no body, no stench, no broken dreams
because you are not here
in this dark place,
just in the light?
It is too bright for me to see;
but the voice I know.

May I reach out
and touch that light,
and in so doing
be a part of life
that knows no pain
of separation from you?
Can you become a part of me,
so that no longer
will I search for you among the dead,
but live with you in your bright sun?
Yes, I feel your presence here.
You did not stay within this cave,
to be a place of sanctuary.
Instead, you opened
up my heart of night
and transformed
it into joy unknown.
Today, your resurrection
means that I, too,
can live a life of hope.
For death will not now hold,
and this tomb
can never be a place
for me to come.
~*Richard L. Elam*

SAVED

In a world of darkness
a light was sent from above,
And in a place of hatred
I felt the warmth of love,
For when You looked at me
You looked inside,
You showed me I had nothing to hide.

And I still feel Your ever lasting love
shining like the sun
from beyond the sky
up above.

And all the things I've ever done wrong
are now just whispers of a forgotten song,
And all my tears are wiped away,
my anger gone with yesterday.

My Lord, You've shown me Heaven,
You've let me feel Your grace,
And when I look into my heart,
I see an angel's face.

~Meagan Doliber

MORE

Today I'll give my heart to You
and close an open door;
I never knew that Your sweet love
could make me want You more,
More than anything on Earth,
much more than anyone,
Your love enfolds me like a glove
and warms me like the sun.

And when You come into my heart
and take my past from me,
I know that You will mold me
into what my life should be;
I give You all my pockets full
of more than life can bring,
I give You all my worldly goods,
for they are only things.

More than this, I give to You
my love and seek to try
to serve You with my all and all
until You bid me die;
I lay my life before You, Lord,
to live for Your sweet Son,
I will love You more than life,
much more than anyone.

~Suze Vanderbeck
4/15/96

SO, WHO'S PERFECT?

There are no perfect spouses,
as yet no perfect life.
We don't have perfect houses,
children, husband, wife.
There is no perfect friendship
and still no perfect town;
for certain not a kinship
of perfection has been found.
There are no perfect people
(least of all with me)
and churches' crooked steeples
are there for all to see.
No one's a perfect teacher,
no country always right.
Failure is a feature
that's always within sight.
But deep within our being
and close upon our heart
a feeling that is freeing,
a notion set apart.
That God took what was perfect
and sacrificed a son,
and thus profoundly affect
the way that we have come.
For now the perfect Stranger
has risen from his sleep;
no more are we in danger
of slipping ever deep.
His awesome restoration
has cast away old skin,
shed new light and direction,
and changed us from within.
No perfection in the mixture
of weather, or our hair,
but God's perfect picture
of love is always there.
Focus on the Author
of all that's good and true,
and even when you falter,
he will be true to you.

~*Richard L. Elam*

THERE ARE NO LIMITS

There are no limits
To what God can do,
He's always been there
For me and for you.

We're surrounded by proof
Of His greatness and His power,
If we only look around us
In any place, at any hour.

He keeps the stars and planets
Spinning on their proper courses,
He controls the blowing of the wind
And all the unseen forces.

We see His majesty reflected
In the mystery of the seas,
In the beauty of the mountains
In the flowers and the trees.

There are no limits
To what God has done,
For to this earth
He sent His only begotten Son.

God will provide for us
Every hour of every day,
In His unexpected
But all-wise way.

He will answer every prayer,
He will meet every need,
He will guide our way
In every thought and deed.

There are no limits
To what God can do,
When you need Him most
He will be there for you.

~*Doris Allen Davis*
1996

A WONDROUS STORY

He was God's firstborn, this little Godly
    child,
Who spent time on earth to teach us for a
    while;
Wrapped in swaddling clothes He came to
    die for sin,.
Not for His own but those of other men's;
He was laid inside a manger on His birthday,
Beneath Him a pillow and a mattress made of
    hay,
Proclaimed by angels who brought news of
    His birth,
Glory to God in the highest, and peace to
    men on earth;
For the first time Almighty God then became
    a man,
Such an event of love we cannot understand,
How our Savior inhabited a body He himself
    had made,
Then willingly died upon a cross, a price for
    sins be paid;
Only a loving God with too much love to
    ever comprehend
Would give His life as ransom to save a
    world of sin;
This is indeed a wondrous story for our ears
    to behold--
A love gift from our God that can't be
    bought or sold.

                    ~*Gary Jenkins*
                    The Servant
                    1995

WHAT IS MAN?

What is man that Thou art mindful?
Pitiful creatures are we;
It seems we always make mistakes,
But through Your love You see.

You see beyond our tear-stained eyes,
beyond our robes so soiled;
You see the blood of Jesus Your Son
and Satan's endeavors foiled.

Our righteousness is as filthy rags,
our hearts were black with sin;
But Jesus' death upon the cross
brought forgiveness deep within.

And when You look upon our hearts,
filthy rags You never see;
Instead the righteousness of Your Son
has made us totally free.

~Patricia A. Behnken
June 17, 1998

GOD'S CREATIONS

Blades of grass waving gently
underneath the breeze,
Whispering pines so big and strong,
all around they gleam.

Shining sun high in the sky,
shedding warmth and light,
Twinkling stars that seem to smile,
peeking through the night.

All these things surrounding us,
bringing peace and love,
Because they are God's creations,
sent to all He loves.

So hold onto these newfound things,
remembering your faith;
For we are His and He is ours,
and with it He brings grace.

~Tracy Tammaro

ANGELS

Angels all dressed in white,
so pure and soft as snow;
Playing all the melodies,
we all love to know.

Soaring high up in the sky,
yet by our sides they stay;
Sharing all of Gods great love,
showing us the way.

We cannot see, but only visualize
these beautiful ones He's sent;
He wants us all to realize,
His time nor love is ever spent;

That He is here with all His love,
to touch our heart and soul;
So we may praise and honor Him,
so everyone will know.

For the day is coming to leave this world,
to join Him in the light;
So, lets join hearts and praise the Lord,
and forever we'll have life.

~Tracy Tammaro

I AM THAT I AM, THE PRESENCE

When I think in my mind through all my life,
three parts of it do appear...
Yesterday, today and tomorrow,
three separate and far, yet near.
When I think of the past: seems far behind,
friends lost in a world of their own,
following dreams their lives have led
and ways that they all have sown.
They are all now very far from me,
their faces I never see;
Their names I hardly ever recall,
and never do they think of me.
When I think of the past, 'tis a time gone by,
the feelings I had then are gone;
The closeness I felt in those bygone days
seem lost in yesterday's dawn.
Today is real now, 'tis today I can feel,
my friends now are still close by,
But someday this today will be in my past,
and feelings will be gone as a sigh;.
The future ahead in my life is to come, those
feelings have not yet started,
The friends I shall meet I've not yet seen ,
and memories have not been imparted.
But thinking of yesterday, long ago past, and
thinking of today how I feel,
and thinking of the future that has not been,
there's something in all that is real.
Through all of my life there is something that
follows from yesterday, to now and
  tomorrow:
In each of the three I feel the presence of
One, who has, does, and will guide through
  all sorrow.

I feel the strong, comforting presence of
   God,
His overpowering love so true;
His fellowship sweet is so fresh to me,
whether past, present or future new.
He has not changed, He's always been there,
He was there then, He's here today;
And I know in my heart I can trust His
   word,
and He'll be here tomorrow, still the
   same.
In all of these days and troublesome times,
when my heart longs to feel the past,
and dreads today, yet fears tomorrow,
I can hold onto the One who lasts;
I can talk to Him, He's followed me through,
He's walked side by side with me;
He's talked with me and led the way
and He's here by my side now with me.
"I Am That I Am," no wonder He says!
I Am is there in my past,
He's here in my present as *I Am*,
and *I Am* is forever to last.
I am ever so grateful for the presence of
   God,
that daily leads me through,
for You my dear Jesus who stays with me,
and Your mercy ever so true.
Make me worthy through Your righteous
   blood,
Your eternity one day to enter;
And let me always be there with You,
Not just yesterday, today, but forever.

                  ~Patricia A. Behnken
                  November 29, 1997

BENEATH THE OLIVE TREE

In a garden in Gethsemane
The Lord Jesus went to pray,
For He knew the time was near
When He would be betrayed.

Peter and James and John
He took with Him there
And asked them to keep watch,
As He went to God in prayer.

As Jesus prayed and struggled,
Knowing the pain He was to bear,
His disciples only slept,
Offering no comfort to Him there.

Earnestly our Savior prayed
Take away this cup from me,
For He knew the price He'd pay
Would be a cross on Calvary.

How sorrowful was His soul,
How great His agony,
As He prayed to His Father
Beneath the olive tree.

Strengthened by an angel
Sent from the Father to His Son,
Jesus answered for all mankind
Not my will, but thine, be done.

~*Doris Allen Davis*
1996

THE RESURRECTION

Twas long ago, in days now past,
my Lord was crucified,
He hung upon a cruel cross,
And in agony He died;

The angry crowds had mocked Him so,
His flesh was torn apart,
And on the cross they nailed Him;
He died of a broken heart.

The blood He shed was shed for me,
the pain He bore for me;
The cross He carried up the hill
so that I'd one day be free.

They placed His body in a tomb;
A stone in front they sealed,
so none could steal the body saying,
"He's risen as God revealed."

But in three days my Lord arose,
in triumph over the grave;
To all believing on His Name
salvation free He gave.
This day He sits on God's right hand,
A place for me He'll prepare;
By grace I'll enter Heaven's gate
and Christ will meet me there.

~Patricia A. Behnken

HIDDEN IN PLAIN VIEW

He comes in quiet whispers,
In the rustling of the leaves,
In the blowing of the wind,
In a cool ocean breeze.

He is the powerful eagle
That soars in it's flight,
He's the fragrance of summer flowers
And the shining stars at night.

We see Him in trees towering
And laden in new snow,
In the beauty of the clouds
And the colors of a rainbow.

He is the unconditional love
Of a father and a mother,
He's the helping hand offered
From one friend to another.

We marvel at a baby's birth
Or the innocence of a child,
We brighten at a warm embrace
Or a friend or stranger's smile.

We delight in the song
That the sparrow sweetly sings,
We look for the falling rain
And the harvest that it brings.

We all become accustomed
To love and beauty that surround,
Accepting without thought or thanks
All God's blessings that abound.

All we take for granted
Not giving credit where it's due,
We fail to see God's presence
Though it is hidden in plain view.

~Doris Allen Davis
1996

I HAVE NEVER SEEN AN ANGEL

Though I have never seen an angel,
I know that they are there,
Keeping watch over me
With great love and great care.

They mark our paths and remind us
Of God's all powerful love,
They guide us as we're on our way
While keeping watch from above.

I feel their presence 'round me
In times of doubt and fear,
And though I cannot see them,
I know that they are near.

Untouched by sin the angels are,
They are pure in heart and deed,
God sends them to protect us
In our times of greatest need.

The angels are God's messengers,
Beautiful spirits we are told,
They are here with us today
Just as in the days of old.

The angels are sustained
By God's almighty power,
His special tasks they perform
On His command at any hour.

May I worship as the angels did
Before the mighty throne
And rejoice when their trumpets sound,
To call me to His home.

Someday I'll see the angels,
What a day that will be!
A time of celebration,
As they sing God's victory.

~Doris Allen Davis
1996

SOMEHOW

As I kneel before the Cross of Sorrow,
I realize He gave me back tomorrow;
I turn around and Jesus do I see,
Somehow I know that He is there for me.

I lift my hand, He reaches back for mine,
I never knew a feeling so divine;
I feel my heart leap upward to the sky,
Somehow, I know that He's the reason why.

And, late at night, when sleep I try to feign,
He seeks me out and calls to me by name;
It's hard to think that He could want me so,
Somehow I know, somehow, my Lord, I
    know.

Somehow He knows my name,
Somehow He feels my pain,
Somehow He wants me for His own.

Somehow He cares for me,
Somehow He sets me free,
Somehow He knows I'm going home.

~*Suze Vanderbeck*
4/15/96

WHY

"Why?" You ask me," Is your God so
 great?"
"Why?" I say.

"Yes," you say," What has He given to this
 Earth?"
"What?" I say, "Well, He put springs into the
 valleys,
That flow amongst the hills,
These springs give drink to every beast of the
 field,
He causes the grass to grow, for the cattle,
He created the trees, where the birds make
 their nests."

"What?" you ask, "What else has He done?"
"What?" I say, "He created the moon and the
 sun,
He made darkness, and it is night,
Which is when the beasts creep about."

"What?" you ask, "What has this God done
 for me?"
"What?" I say, "Look around you,
He put land here, for you to live on,
He has sent you food, for you to eat,
He has sent you water, for you to drink,
And He didn't stop there;
Look into the sky; see the birds,
Flying through the winds?
Look there, see the flowers, and all the
 beautiful creatures, and
Most importantly, look into the mirror,
For God, has given you life."

"So, You ask me why is my God so great?
I think you can figure that out now." :-)
 ~*Dorothy Marie Jackson*
 5/3/98

TEARS IN HIS EYES

When I come to the river and I look to the sky,
when I seek out the Father and I ask Him, "Lord, why?"
When I look in the water, I will see my Lord cry,
for His blood's in the river, and that's why He died.

I was washed in the river,
I was washed in the blood,
and the blood He has given
covers me like a flood;
Now I'm just like an angel,
pure and bathed in His light,
Gonna live through the ages,
'cuz I'm gonna live right.

When I see my sweet Jesus at the river's end,
I know He'll deliver my soul round the bend;
He is more than a Savior, He is my best friend,
When I call out His sweet name, His love He will send.

I am washed in the river,
I am washed in the blood,
My soul is delivered
and I'm cleansed from the mud;
When I look toward sweet Jesus,
there are tears in His eyes,
for His blood's in the river
and for me He did die.

~Suze Vanderbeck
8/19/96

WITH THANKSGIVING

All of my life I have been waiting for the
right time to tell You how much You mean
   to me;
You have helped me through so much more
than I've realized, I know You
   can see;
I go through my ups and downs, but still
You stand by my side helping me up when I
   seem to fall;
So many times I scrape my knees, I cry and
You always hear me call,
I call out Your name... " Oh Lord, please
help me fight this pain, it has hurt me so."
You seem to be the only one in my life who's
   never said no;
I want to show You my appreciation, I want
to give my whole life to You,
but instead You remind me of how, even
though times may be hard, I still have a job
   to do.
I have come to realize that every soul on this
   earth was put here for
some kind of purpose, that I do know;
Every day I search in hope that I will find
mine and then my heart will grow.
Again, I thank You Lord, until I find my
place in life, I thank You.

~Lana St. John

THANK YOU LORD

Lord, Thou hast given me great things,
Thou hast filled my heart to overflowing;
The doors are wide open for me to enter,
Thy words of righteousness are calling me in.

Thy glory before me, this day I can see,
Thy blessing of love hast enfolded me;
My eyes are now opening and begin to
   behold,
my lips learning to speak and my heart to be
   bold.

All gifts are from Thee, Lord, I've found,
Without Thee I'd perish and drown
in all the cares and pleasures of earth;
But I'm saved and find peace in this new
   birth.

The fire of Thy Spirit upon me descends,
and wisdom and knowledge to me become
   friends;
The strength and the power of Thy holy
   prayer
lets me know I am heard and the answer is
   there.

Thank you dear Lord, for all You have
   given
and for when I'll be there to join You in
   Heaven;
And thank you now for the grace You give,
that while I'm still here I can truly live.

~Patricia A. Behnken

ANOTHER CHANCE

New doors are beginning to open,
Old doors are closed behind,
All new and great experiences
Capture each part of my mind.

The stillness and quiet of study
Lets the presence of Jesus come in,
And the triumph of passing a test
Gives the glory to Jesus again.

I know now that I have a new chance
To begin where I stopped in the past;
My desire to advance to success
Is now coming to pass at last.

The Lord's work? It always continues,
People come my direction each day;
With God's help and all of His blessing,
I can help them to find Jesus' way.

And each time I hear of a need
That I know needs an answer today,
The Lord lets me know in my heart
That He'll answer each time that I pray.

Thank you God for all Your great glory,
For all that before me I see,
And for all hidden things in the future
That You have now planned just for me.

~Patricia A. Behnken

NATURAL LOVE

The fruit was gathered,
vineyards bare,
orchards were picked
prosperity rare.

Happy hearts filled
with abundance and more,
after much hardship
a harvest galore.

The sea too was yielding,
for fishermen near,
enough to keep catching
for well over a year.

Bees flying around,
the clover and such,
America the plenty,
God loves you so much.

~Alfred N. Renshaw
Isaiah 40:31

THANKSGIVING

T　is for thanking the Lord everyday
H　is for happiness to walk in His way
A　is for answering to His every call
N　is for near to the cross we must fall
K　is for knees where we are when we pray
S　is for seeking the Lord every day
G　is for goodness on us He bestows
I　is the interest in each one He shows
V　is for victory when in us He lives
I　is for infinite joy that He gives
N　is for new birth, the gift from above
G　is for growing in His precious love

~Patricia A. Behnken

FROM GOD'S PRECIOUS HAND

Man's resources are limited
But God has abundant supply,
All the things man cannot give
Our merciful God will provide.

He will give us all we need
If only we let Him prevail,
He offers the riches of Glory
For His children He will not fail.

Many messengers and means
He uses, our gifts to deliver,
Though He is always the source
We may not recognize the Giver.

Often in our complacent way
Our blessings we fail to see,
The many simple pleasures
He bestows upon you and me.

The love of a family,
The table at which we eat,
A kind word from a stranger,
A new friend that we meet.

The comfort we are offered,
Nature's beauty that we behold,
Every smile that comes our way,
Every hand that we hold.

With every breath that we take,
For every life that we touch,
God's work we should always do
For He has given us so much,

Never let there be a doubt,
More in number than the sand
The many blessings that we have
Are from God's precious hand.

~Doris Allen Davis
1996

HOPE

COMFORT

†

AND

ENCOURAGEMENT

PATHWAYS OF MY JOURNEY
Dedicated in loving memory of
Dawn R. Reed 1962-1995

I woke up this morning and opened my eyes
To look at my world with thoughts so young,
Wondering at each blurring sight to behold;
In my mother's arms, my journey had begun.
My first little steps were so trembling and weak
I stumbled and fell, but my courage grew strong,
So I got back up to start on my way;
As my journey continued, the pathway seemed long.
The path I first took was twisted and gnarled,
And I struggled through rocks and ruts in the road,
Though the pathway was wide, it was hard to take,
And the burden I carried seemed too heavy a load.
Once it seemed I was coming to the end of my way,
And the path took a drop, then nothing in sight,
As I drew closer, I found a surprise:
A refreshing stream, fruitful trees and sky so bright.
The presence of God was filling the air,
He took hold of my hand and led me across
To an old narrow but beautiful pathway of life,
My burden was traded for a small simple cross.

I began my new pathway with hope in my
  heart,
I continued my journey with Christ as my
  Guide,
No longer did I have to travel alone--
My Saviour walked with me, close by my
  side.
Though sometimes frightening things would
  occur,
My comforter stood near me against any
  threat,
When tired and weary and so dry from thirst,
A stream from a Rock was a clear, running
  faucet.
When looking ahead toward high mountains
  to climb,
I wondered how possible to keep from a fall,
But nearing the bottom, to start up the side,
There were hands there to help me, if only I'd
  call.
A few more miles are needed to take
To finish my journey at the close of the day,
A city, a mansion and friendship, so dear
Will be waiting beyond at the end of the way.
I'll fall at the throne of our King, so great,
To praise Him forever in skies ever bright,
With joy overwhelming in Heavenly realm
Forever to live with everything right.
No sickness, no sorrow, no aging, nor death,
But peace and love and joy evermore:
Looking ahead to such rapture divine
Will give peace to cross over to eternity's
  shore.

~*Patricia A. Behnken*
1993

HOPE

When walls seem to crumble in on you,
And your life seems crashing in,
You struggle to hold onto something strong:
It is hope that you feel within.

Hope is all you feel in your heart,
As tears roll down your face,
Hope says that everything is not all lost
--that soon you'll be blessed with God's
   grace.

God's grace will see you through,
As hope comes surging enmass,
And the hope you feel turns into faith,
And you know in your heart this will pass.

Then hope begins to imagine new dreams
And makes you plan anew,
Then happiness swells within your heart
With refreshing peace renewed.

~Patricia A. Behnken
June 2, 1998

I KNOW I CAN

For I know that in me (that is, in my flesh,)
dwelleth no good thing: for to will is
present with me; but how to perform
that which is good I find not.
—Romans 7:18

Lord, I have a problem,
I'm not sure what it is!
Could I tell it all to You?
Can You show me what I miss?
You see I'm confused,
I'm not sure what I want,
I want to live to please You,
but whenever I try, I can't;
For a while I'm ok,
then things begin to happen,
Just when I feel happy,
my spirits then get dampened;
I know I'm not perfect,
I've got a long way to go,
But I sure plan on trying,
no matter if I'm low;
It may seem I have no fight left,
but I'll try my best to win,
I'll need You to help me,
cause without You I'll never make it in!
So, Lord, please help me,
 just give me another try,
I know I can do it,
with You on my side.

~*Renee M. Malone*
1988

THE SHIELD OF SCARLET

For years the world held me
In the palm of it's hand,
I was there for it's bidding
To respond to it's command.

I took pleasure in things external,
Never looking deep within,
I wandered without purpose
In my life of sin.

When I thought that I was lost
With no place left to go,
Little did I understand
How God loved me so.

He loved me so -- He gave His son
The ultimate sacrifice,
So that I, His precious child,
Might have everlasting life.

Then I was touched by God's hand,
I felt His embrace,
I heard His word,
I was saved by His grace.

Now my burdens He carries,
My sorrows He relieves,
My petitions He hears,
My praise He receives.

Now the world cannot touch me,
For I am covered by a shield,
A shield freely offered
Upon Calvary's Hill.

The shield is of scarlet
And was given just for me,
That precious shield of scarlet
Has finally set me free. ~*Doris Allen Davis*
1998

HE'S TASTED THE TEARS

He walked the streets of Jerusalem teaching as
    He'd go,
Telling of a way of life people needed to know;
He never told a lie nor did He any wrong,
yet suffered so much injustice wherever He'd gone;
Lies were told about Him and of what He'd done,
He was rejected by the leaders and almost
    everyone;
Sometimes in self pity I think no one cares,
It's then I'm reminded: He's tasted the tears.

Through the death of a loved one sometimes I've
    cried out,
Thinking no one knows what my hurt is all about;
It's a part of life with which we all have to deal,
And you can be assured Jesus knows how we feel;
Standing at the tomb of Lazarus where his body
    was kept,
I've read in the Bible it was there Jesus wept;
Sometimes in self pity I think no one cares,
It's then I'm reminded: He's tasted the tears.

I have felt forsaken as sometimes Christians do,
it's then I'm reminded of what our Lord went
    through;
Hanging upon the cross He cried out in agony,
My God! My God! why hast Thou forsaken me?
Of Jesus suffering I can't comprehend
or why He so willingly suffered for my sin;
But one thing's for certain I know He really cares,
And I've no doubt at all: He's tasted the tears.

~Gary Jenkins
The Servant
1/23/90

Luke 23:37
John 11:35
Matthew 27:46

WITH JESUS NEVER ALONE

Sometimes life seems hard, Lord–
The things we must go through,
Sometimes we wonder why, Lord
Paths lead where they do;
Sometimes our feeble legs bend
Beneath the load they carry,
Our hearts seems to melt then,
And we become so weary;
But then I think of where You went
That day You walked for me,
The load You carried, your legs bent,
You stumbled and fell for me;
I think about the tears You cried,
Your heart was broken in two,
I think about the way You died–
Your friends had forsaken You;
So, I'll let You help me carry my load,
I will never alone abide,
Upon life's very weary road
You'll always be at my side.

~Patricia A. Behnken
June 17, 1994

TRIALS

Lord, my life is a whirlwind,
I know not up nor down,
I know not what the answers are,
I'm just spinning round and round.

The winds are tossing me to and fro,
they toss me left and right;
I struggle to hold onto Thy hand
and to keep You in my sight.

Troubled clouds, dark and bleak
keep moving across the sky;
They try to hide You from my view,
to divide You from my eye.

But in my heart I keep holding on,
though the dark trials seem as night;
I know that I'm not hidden from You,
for Your eye sees through darkness as light.

I know that beyond my limited view
the storm will one day be past,
and joy and peace just wait there beyond,
when I come to the end of this test.

~Patricia A. Behnken
September 30, 1995

TEARS FROM HEAVEN
Dedicated to C.M. and J.M.

Forgive me, Lord,
For I have sinned,
There's so much to say
I can't even begin.

Will You give me Your mercy
As I beg and I cry?
When You say You forgive me
I wonder why.

So I kneel down before You,
Seeking Your grace,
I'm begging for penance
With tears on my face.

You say, "My child,
I shall always love thee,
Look up to the sky,
Do you know what you see?

You may see clouds
You may see rain,
You may see endless days of pain,
You may see dark
You may see light,
You may see stars:
Some dull, some bright,
You may see a dove
Flying overhead,
You may see blue hues
You may see red.

Look up to the heavens
And sky's all you'll see,
Look into your soul
And that's where I'll be."

And as He turns to go
I beg and I plea,
"Please, Lord, stay,
I need You with me."

Gently He laughs
And smiles, then He
Whispers a promise,
"I shall never leave thee."

~Meagan Doliber

FREE SKIES

When there are days of endless pain
And all I can do is cry,
Although its hard to raise my head
I look up and watch the sky.

Let the sun set on my anger,
Let the wind blow away my fears,
Let the clouds disperse with my hate,
Let the rain wash away my tears.

And when the sky is blue and the sun is
    warm,
My soul will fly away free.
And when the Lord lifts me from this world.
I'll be happy to know I'm me.

~Meagan Doliber

PRAYER FOR PEACE (OF MIND)

An apology is due, to You.
I cannot bow my head
or lift my eyes
or fear, or dread
the power of Your being.
I cannot accept the Truth
men set forth in Your name.
But just the same
I cannot deny, or I
would have no reason to be.

You see
there are only truths,
not Truth for me;
but only You know and so
I turn to You as one
who believes
in the virtue of a relationship
and leaves
the rest to You.

~Richard L. Elam

I WILL COMFORT THEE

When thou shalt tremble
I will overshadow thee with My wings,
I shall hide thee in the secret place of
my pavilion and cause thee to sing.
Even the youth
shall grow weary and faint,
But they that wait upon the Lord
shall renew their strength;
In times of trouble
I will not be far from thee, but near,
So that when thou callest upon Me
I will surely hear;
I will keep thy foot
that thou shalt surely not slip,
For in the day of thy call unto Me
My mercy shalt hold thee up;
Fear thou not, be not dismayed,
for I am thy God, giving thee strength and
help, for by My righteousness, I will
uphold thee with My right hand.

> Arrangement of scriptures
> ~Patricia A. Behnken
> August 12, 1994

Seven scripture chapters in order of use:
    Psalm 91, Psalm 149, Psalm 27,
    Isaiah 40, Psalm 20, Psalm 94,
    Isaiah 41

WHEN YOU DON'T FEEL LIKE SINGING

There are times when you don't feel like
   singing a song--
When emotions go deep and all the things
   that go wrong
Are more traumatic than just errors and
   bumbles
And the pathway you walk seems more like
   the jungles.

In those times the heart wants to silently cry,
To reach out in silence to the Savior who's
   nigh;
He alone hears the cry from your heart
And feels the deepest of pains and the
   enemy's dart.

Then in silence you can reach out to hold His
   hand,
To know He is with you in this weary land
And feel the comfort and wonderful peace
   from above,
Knowing you are resting in His precious
   love.

~Patricia A. Behnken
May 14, 1996

TIMES OF TWILIGHT

In every lifetime there are times of twilight,
days when the path ahead seems so unclear;
Times when we feel abandoned or
    discouraged,
so sure that no one sees our pain or fear.

At night we lie and tremble in the darkness,
covered with self-pity and despair;
Wishing for the light that hails the sunrise,
yet dreading what we may find waiting there.

Still in the darkest night a light can flicker,
growing brighter with each whispered word
    of prayer.
Each tiny step of faith can lead us closer
to a place where hope and trust replace
    despair.

For no matter how dim the misty rays of
    twilight,
and no matter how unclear the path we tread,
and no matter that we sometimes grow
    discouraged,
God's love will lead us through what lies
    ahead.

~Donna M. Givens

WALKING IN THE UNKNOWN

Walking through the shadows
toward places so unknown;
The darkness all around me,
frightening, tone for tone.

Taking each step with carefulness,
watching every move,
so as not to fall into a hole,
stranded, no place to go.

When suddenly appears a light
from somewhere up above;
It lights my path, the fear is gone,
I'm surrounded by lasting love.

Thank you Lord for showing me
life can turn around;
With You always by my side,
I know I will not drown.

~*Tracy Tammaro*

TRUST

I was trying to stay alert, the battle was hard and I felt like I was dying. Inside I had a spirit that said I have to keep trying and trust in my Savior. He has not left me nor forsaken me; He will see me through. Oh yes, I might hurt and I might cry, but my God will see me through. He has carried and helped me many times; so I know He will help me this time, if I put my trust in Him.

~Margaret A. Burchfield

OH WHAT A JOURNEY

Even as a child I started out on a journey. I was bowed down by bitterness and hate. This journey was not much fun; I cried a lot and begged for mercy everyday of my childhood. Then, I married and still wished for a better life; it was all downhill. I
then met Jesus, and my journey became great; He's my friend, my keeper, and most of all my Savior. This journey I take will lead me all the way to Heaven; and on the way I have peace, joy, and happiness, because of God and His mercy.
        Oh what a journey!

~Margaret A. Burchfield

ON DEATH ROW

*And the devil that deceived them was cast
into the lake of fire and brimstone,
where the beast and the false prophet are,
and shall be tormented day and night
forever and ever. Rev.20:10*

He stands before the jury–tall, haughty and proud,
But when they say, "He's guilty," I hear him scream so loud;
For crimes he has committed, he's worthy now of death,
The judge begins to sentence, while everyone holds their breath;
The sentence now is given, he'll die after several days,
Nothing can be done now, even if he'd change his ways;
The guard now leads him outside, he cannot get away,
He leads him back to prison, where he'll be for several days;
But when the days are ended, the guard will bring him out,
He'll lead him down the corridor, his enemies will shout;
He'll take him to the chamber, where death will come to call,
And his life will then be ended right before his victims all.
The devil is our enemy, he torments day and night,
It seems we're always victims, he's always there to fight;
But one day in God's presence, he stood before the throne,
And God pronounced the sentence, and the devil's overthrown;

He only walks the earth now, seeking whom
  he may devour,
But deep inside his being, he knows he's
  waiting for the hour;
God pronounced the sentence: eternal torment
  in the flames,
The devil now is waiting, his place won't be
  regained;
And one day in our presence the devil will be
  led out
And as he walks before us, we'll all be able to
  shout;
The accuser of the brethren will seem so small
  and weak
His power will be taken and his victims all will
  speak;
One by one, we'll tell about all the things he
  did,
Of all the times he abused us and tempted us to
  sin;
We'll tell of all he tried to steal, the things he
  took away,
And one by one, we'll get to come, and all will
  have their say;
All of us are witnesses to his evil deeds,
There will be no mercy for him and none to
  intercede;
All will know he's guilty, and he'll be sent
  away,
And the sentence will be carried out upon the
  judgement day;
So when you feel discouraged, disheartened or
  just low,
Encourage yourself in Jesus, because the
  devil's on death row!

~ *Patricia A. Behnken*
January, 1998

CLOSER TO YOU

All I want is to be closer to You–
To know You are standing at my side,
To feel Your presence in all I do
And know You're there each moment I'm
    tried.

As I take each step, Your hand I hold
And know You're with my every move–
To feel the Potter's hand as You mold
And know Your master craft is true.

You know that I can't understand,
The days before me are unsure,
And though this time's not as I planned,
I know Your love for me is pure.

So help me each day and guide me through,
Give me strength and courage and faith,
And let me feel Your overwhelming love
And draw me closer to You today.

~Patricia A. Behnken
December 2, 1994

THE HAND

The hand on my shoulder,
so tender, so dear,
It says I love you and
yes, I am here.

I'm here for you when
inside you cry,
I know your hurtings and
each time you sigh.

It may be silent to others' ears,
but my ear, not deaf
hears each silent cry and
hides you in the cleft.

~Patricia A. Behnken
March, 1995

KEEP WALKING

I walk along this lonely path
in the dark of night;
The wind is whispering a lowly tune,
the leaves scatter with fright.

What's up ahead and down the road?
One can only guess;
Do we keep walking or just stand still?
How do we know what's best?

As time goes by the night air chills,
the light seems far away;
You try to move, but your feet are still,
and like the trees you sway.

The dark, cold night rages around you,
but still you know the truth;
You must be calm and move ahead,
for there's nowhere else to go.

~*Tracy Tammaro*

OUR GUIDE IN LIFE

Silence we hear in the still of night
as we lay our heads to rest;
Sleep, precious ones, don't you cry,
for we all know the test;
He will be there to guide your way,
though you may not know;
He'll carry you through the hardest times,
He'll never let you go;
Even if you understand,
or even if you don't,
He'll be there to help you through,
just believe and trust His word;
For one day soon He'll take us all,
He'll come forth in the night;
But have no fear, oh precious ones,
for He will be your light;
Trust in God, have faith my dear,
and you will know in time,
The greatest gift He'll give to you
will be Eternal Life.

~Tracy Tammaro

JESUS YOU KNOW

Jesus, You know my every trial,
I know You always hear;
And Jesus I know, in my hardest hours,
That You will always be near.

Each trial I face won't be alone,
You'll be right by my side,
And all my fears will vanish away
When I, in You will confide.

You alone will be right here
When it seems no one's with me,
You will never be leaving my side,
Standing watch and guarding me.

You said to cast our cares upon You
Because You care for us,
And if we trust in what You say,
You then shall surely bless.

I give You myself and trust in You,
Though this pathway I must trod,
I know I'll be safe and You'll protect,
For You are the Son of God.

~Patricia A. Behnken
December 28, 1994

JESUS LOVES YOU

When times get hard
and there's long hours too,
just lift up your heart and remember
–Jesus loves you!
He'll brighten your day
and bring blessings anew,
If only you'll try to remember
–Jesus loves you!
His promise is health
and there's new pathways, too,
If you'll trust in Him and remember
Jesus loves you!
He'll remain your friend
and He'll always be true,
If you'll walk with Him and remember
Jesus loves you!
God's hand is upon you
and He'll bring you right through;
So keep up your faith and remember
Jesus loves you!

~Patricia A. Behnken
March, 1974

THE RACE

The little boy said to his daddy, I've something I'd like to ask...
Last night I dreamed I was in a race, but I couldn't run very fast;
There were lots of miles to run and I was way behind,
And the energy to catch up I just couldn't seem to find,
I was getting so tired and I had to slow my pace,
There were a lot of miles and I wanted to finish the race;
Then I really goofed and turned down the wrong road,
I hadn't paid attention to the way the signs had showed,
I made so many mistakes and kept falling farther back,
The incentive to keep on trying I was beginning to lack;
Then I felt a hand on my shoulder and a sweet voice in my ear,
That said don't worry my son, your Father is right here;
A power came upon me like I've never felt before,
Then like on an eagle's wings I began to soar;
Never once again did my feet ever touch the ground,
Surprised even greater when I had won the race I found;
Daddy why do you think I'd have such a dream?
Do you think it was from Jesus, if so what does it mean?

The first part is life and the physical shape
    you're in,
The many wrong turns you'll make because
    of your sin,.
The voice was the Lord's, He was the one
    who spoke,
He had lightened your burden and lifted up
    your yoke;
His son sat in the wheelchair as dad bent
    down to speak,
The race is the Lord's and He has given you
    a peek;
One day your legs won't be crooked, He will
    make them strong,
And carry you on the wings of an eagle, for
    to Him you belong.

~Gary Jenkins
The Servant
2/20/90

MY LITTLE LAMB

Little lamb you think you're all alone,
But I've watched your footsteps all along,
You've walked through thickets, I've see you hide,
But I've always been there at your side,
And you've not been hidden to me;

Your feet have been muddy and bloody too,
Sharp rocks have cut you, hurting you,
You've cried and thought no one had heard,
Your heart was pierced and teary eyes blurred,
But your sobbing's been heard by me;

You've only cried alone it seems,
But little lamb I've been there in your dreams,
Dreams that seem all shattered and empty,
Mountains too tall and deep dark seas,
But search your dreams and find me;

Little lamb I'm reaching out for you,
And waiting for you to reach out too,
You're not alone, for I am here,
Waiting to dry your every tear,
Look up little lamb, see me;

I understand, I've been there too,
They pierced my flesh through and through,
I gave my life upon the cross,
So I could find my little lamb lost,
Reach out little lamb to me;

I died and rose that you might live,
Your sins forgiven, this gift I give,
Reach out and take my love by faith,
And I will give you mercy and grace,
Give your heart little lamb to me;

Little lamb my love is ever strong,
And little lamb, my arm is long
And able to lift you if you come
And you accept God's only Son,
Open your heart little lamb to me;

I will lift you out from under despair
And heal your wounds and bless you there
And give you peace and joy within,
And comfort will come and new life begin,
Reach out little lamb for me.

I am reaching out for you...
Because I love you...
And you'll never be alone
If you reach out to me,
I am here....................Jesus.

~Patricia A. Bayless Behnken
Written for and dedicated to
Gretchen Kidd
Nov. 2, 1997

BRIGHTER SKIES

God woke you this morning, brushing the
  hair back from your eyes,
Now all your days ahead will have much
  brighter skies;
The Lord knows how I'll miss you and of
  how much I've prayed,
Longing to have you with me ,wishing you
  could have stayed;
I know you'll like it in heaven, and that's
  where you must be,
But I still love and miss you, and it sure is
  hard on me;
I'm so very thankful to God for the time that
  we spent,
He alone knows the differences in this life
  you meant;
You brought so much happiness, more than
  you ever knew,
The years we had together seem like so very
  few;
I'll never forget you for as long as I may live,
You were so very special as was the love you
  give;
Someday I'll get to see you and we'll never
  have to part,
That's the aspiration that soothes this broken
  heart;
You'll always be on my mind until it happens
  then,
And I will be rejoicing when we're together
  again;
Yes I know God woke you this morning with
  a smile upon your face,
For there isn't any sorrow in heaven, it's
  never had a place;

When I lay me down to finally breathe my last,
I'll no longer be lonely, like I've been in the past;
I'll see those brighter skies, and walk those streets of gold,
Where there isn't any sickness and no one ever grows old;
For now I wait in expectation, longing to be laid to rest,
Then may God please grant me this my last request,
To see Him wake you one morning, brushing the hair back from your eyes,
And walk the golden streets with us, while seeing His brighter skies.

~Gary Jenkins
The Servant
02/12/92

A LETTER TO MOMMY AND DADDY
Dedicated to Baby Fritz

Dear Mommy and Daddy,

Hello! I miss you even though I never really had a chance to see you. I know you miss me too. I wish I could have stayed to get to know you better, but I had to come here.

This place is nice, I'm having a great time. It's called Heaven. I really love it here, and I want you to come here some day, too.

There's a man here who loves me more than I can imagine. He says I'll be here forever, and I don't mind at all! His name is Jesus, and He died just for me (and you too). His Dad is really nice. He gave me Jesus to talk to, so I'm never lonely. He says hi and sends His love. He says that there's a place here for you. There's a place for everyone! And He's waiting for you.

Mommy I know you're sad that I'm not down there with you anymore, and Daddy I know you are upset, too; but please don't be. I'm happy here, I know you will be, too. Please don't be mad at God, He needs me here, and He knows that, with Him, you can handle my leaving.

I was only with you for a while. I'll always treasure those few precious memories. But I'll see you again! Please remember that! I miss you and love you always!   With love, Your Daughter.

~Lindsey Ingram

"Whoever believes in the Son has eternal life, but whoever rejects the Son will not see life, of God's wrath remains on him."
John 3:36

REGRETS, BUT WITH HOPE

Mom, oh Mom, you were getting ready to
die. I didn't even try, cause I thought,
"My mom won't really die."

And then time passed by fast, and it was time
for you to go away. I didn't rush or even try
cause I thought, "My mom won't really die."

I had life's things I thought were pushing and
important, so I didn't rush and didn't even
try, cause I thought my mom surely wouldn't
die.

And then to my surprise, my mom shut her
eyes, and I couldn't even cry. Cause I
thought my mom wouldn't really die.

~Margaret A. Burchfield

Sometimes our hearts won't permit us to
believe that we are going to lose someone
valuable to us–a form of protection our
bodies provide. Afterward, Satan tries to
make us feel guilty. But Jesus understands
and will give us peace and comfort if we
allow Him to.

We have the hope when someone is saved
that we will see them again in Heaven. My
mom was a Christian and I know she went to
Heaven. I didn't get to say good-bye to her
here, but I will get to say hello again to her
when I reach Heaven some day.

~Margaret A. Burchfield.

PUT YOUR HAND IN HIS HAND

There's someone there to love you
When you think you are unloved,
There's someone there to talk to
If you'll look to God above.

Don't despair over your failings
When you are weak or when you fall,
For He is there to lift you up
So you will rise above it all.

When you're down or discouraged
And you carry a heavy load,
He's always there to guide you
Down life's winding, twisting road.

When you give in to temptation
And from His teaching do stray,
You need only look to Him
He will light the darkened way.

When you're tired and you're weary
God will give you rest,
When you look to Him in faith
Your life He'll surely bless.

Rich and bountiful blessings,
Peace and joy and serenity,
And everlasting life with Him,
He will provide for you and me.

Your desire for earthly treasures
Can in no way satisfy,
The secret to contentment
Is to let the Lord supply.

And this He will surely do
And you'll shine in His light,
If you come to Him in trust
Walk by faith and not by sight.

You need not fear the future
For as He guided in the past,
He will always be the Savior,
His love will forever last.

Just put your hand in His hand,
You'll feel His presence there,
Put your hand in His hand,
You'll find comfort in His care.

~*Doris Allen Davis*
1996

I BELIEVE

The Lord is my salvation,
He walks with me all the way;
He is my strength and courage,
as I struggle through the day.

When I am restless or uneasy,
He sets my troubled mind at ease.
In anguish and in sorrow
He offers serenity and peace.

He see my tears of grief
and dries them with His touch;
He calms my anxious spirit,
when my burden seems too much.

And though I'm far from perfect,
I am sure He loves me still,
and as long as I believe,
I believe He always will.

~Donna M. Givens

LOOK BEYOND

Beyond the darkest cloud
there lies a bright blue sky.
Beyond the longest night
there will be a new sunrise.

A peaceful valley waits
just beyond the highest hill.
Beyond the raging river
are waters quiet and still.

Beyond the rocky road
that we each must journey down,
there lies a golden pathway
where love and peace abound.

So as you journey through this life,
when you feel you can't go on,
look past whatever lies ahead
and you'll find what lies beyond.

~Donna M. Givens

FEARS AREN'T THE SAME

Demon Death would stalk nearly everyday,
Whispering words of horror all along the way:
"You can't outrun me, no matter how you try,
You'll be in my clutches on the day you die."
These were his claims he'd hiss into my ears,
Making my life miserable with all kinds of fears.

Then someone gave me a book with hope inside;
It told of a Savior who had been crucified,
That fear could be cast out only by perfect love,
The reason God came from His home above.
There's not any reason to worry or to fret,
for the debts of sin Jesus has already met.

Death may come around sometimes during the day,
But I now quote the scriptures to scare him away.
Now his faint whispers I know are just a lie,
and I will be with Jesus on the day I die.
Jesus is my Lord and Savior, Him I now proclaim,
since He came into my life, my fears aren't the same.

~Gary Jenkins
The Servant

A JOYFUL MORN
*...Weeping may endure for a night, but joy
cometh in the morning.*~Psalm 30:5

Clouds of gray overshadowed the earth,
And sadness upon me reigned,
My life was empty, my mind was tossed,
My spirit was almost drained;
Why was everything happening to me?
Why did I feel so lost?
My heart was so sad, my body racked with
  pain,
Never knew life without Jesus had such cost;
But when I came to the end of my "rope"
And I called upon His name,
The heavy burdens I had laden on me
Were gone and nothing seemed the same;
Where sadness had been, true happiness came,
A joy I had not known,
My life was changed, my spirit was free
Like a bird from its cage had flown;
The night had been long and darkness so bleak
And emptiness all around,
But when I found Jesus the morning shown
  bright,
And great happiness did abound;
When light comes in the darkness must flee,
And all becomes clear as the day;
Jesus is the truth and He is the light
And Jesus is the way;
When the night is so dark and you're heavy of
  heart,
Just open your spirit to learn,
Jesus will take all your weeping away
And bring you a joyful morn.

~Patricia A. Behnken
January 14, 1998

FROM DEATH TO LIFE

I remember it all so well, like it was yesterday: the beginning, the end, or the near end.

"I am so alone! Nothing left," I think to myself as the sadness and sorrow sink deeper and deeper into my being; taking over my soul. "How do things come to be this way?" I wonder aloud to myself. Yes, to myself, as there is no one else around me. No one to care, no one to love me; no one.

"I know there is only one way left...the only way to stop the misery," I am thinking to myself, as I sit on the ocean shore staring out over miles of what seems nothingness; just water. Water that has more life in it than the life within myself. I feel as though I am already dead, no life, not worthy of living.

"You are someone special. You are my daughter!" I hear this voice like thunder come out of nowhere. I turn to look for the voice, but no one is there. "I must be dreaming. No one is out here. I am all alone." I look again out over the ocean....then up to the sky. "Lord," I pray, "Please forgive me for what I am about to do. There just isn't anything left for me. This is the only way to make things right. Please understand!"

"My darling child, you don't understand." Another voice, like the last one; but different, soft, and low, like a whisper in my ear. Yet again, no one was there.

"Now I know I am crazy, just like everyone has said of me! I don't deserve love or happiness. I am nothing!" The tears flow; again I pray, "Oh Lord, my God, please forgive me! Forgive me for all I have done and for what I am to do. The only thing I can do!" I then laugh at myself. "Why am I doing this? Praying like this? Why do I think God would listen to someone like me?" I walk out to the water, put my feet in, as I say to myself, "I know it is what must be." A little further, waves splashing

(Continued)

at my legs. "Not much longer," I tell myself.

"Why do you say you believe in Me yet you believe you are worth nothing?" That voice, again in my ear. I am in the water, alone, no one near me. Yet, there is a voice, speaking to me. I shout, "I don't need anyone, just as no one needs me! Why are you doing this? Just let me die!"

"My child, you still don't understand." I reply, "No one cares, I understand that! I am a sinner, not worthy of living. I don't need anyone!" I cry, as tears stream down my face.

"Ah, child, but you do. You cried out for help, not only in words, but also in your heart. And, in your hesitation."

"I don't know why you say I asked for help. All I want is to die. I don't need help with that. I asked for forgiveness, not for help!"

"My dear child, when you called upon My name, you called for help. When you cried out in your heart, you cried out for help. And, in your hesitation, in the water, you awaited help. I am always with you, watching over you, carrying you through trials you could not go through on your own." I replied, " I was on my own and that is what brought me here today."

"Remember the man who had a dream? Footprints in the sand?"
"Yes," I replied. "Those were My footprints." Said the Lord.

"Then, if You were always with me, why is my life as it is? You say you've walked with me, carried me through, and watched over me. Then why am I going through this hell and ready to end my life?"

"My child, this is what you don't understand. I have done all these things and still you wandered in your own direction; and still I remained with you, waiting for you to take the hand I offered you. You believed that I AM, but you didn't believe with your heart. Nor did you believe that I CAN."

"Lord, I have always wanted to be like You, but I never could be. I am a sinner, fallen to

(Continued)

temptation, now walking alone because of my sins. There seems no way to turn back what I've done."

"My child, don't first search with thine eyes, for they are blind. Search with thine heart which is open; which I opened for you. Then thine eyes will be delivered from blindness. You have sinned, fallen to temptation, but also asked for forgiveness in Thy Sons name, the Lord Jesus Christ, thus you were forgiven." "How can I be forgiven as I am still a sinner?" I asked.

"Precious child, you still only search with thine eyes. As you walked into the water, you asked for forgiveness. Thou asked in the name of Jesus, thou shall receive. You are My child and I love you. My Son was put to death for your sins then resurrected for your salvation. You need to believe in that and also in My Son. Thus is why I say you must first search with thine heart and only then will you be able to see with thine eyes."

"Oh Lord, how could I ever be so blind to all the things you offered? You were there with me at all times and told me thy ways, but I never listened with my heart, only deaf ears. How do I get back what I've missed and all I've lost?"

"Go now My child, be a testimony in My name and for the Lord Jesus Christ. Follow My word, practice and believe in My word. Thus by this do the Lord's will and thou shall forever live, even after the worldly death."

From that day on, I did as the Lord instructed. I searched with my heart and found the beauty through my eyes. I cannot say that there have not been trials along the way. I can say that I reached out and held onto the hand that was offered me. The Lord's hand. And, He is with me always, I know......

.........Just like footprints in the sand.

Fiction Story
~*Tracy Tammaro*
February 18, 1998

STOP

THINK

✝

AND

CONSIDER

PROBLEMS IN THE GARDEN

Am I really hypocritical,
when I say some larger truths exist?
Do I go against my friends and all,
or should I take temptations to resist?
When Eve and Adam hastened then the fall,
should they have simply vanished into mist,
taken all their genes and dust recall,
betray us everyone like Judas' kissed?
Instead, the world with paradoxes crawl,
every permutation has a twist;
and I must try to scale that heightened wall,
since that serpent's voice came up and hissed.

~Richard L. Elam

SIN SICK

In someone else the sin I see,
amazing its vitality;
glaring wrong, that Pharisee
seeking visibility;
But sin is never clear to me,
I never give it company,
it's here temporarily;
Surely, you can now agree
that I am pure compared to thee.

~Richard L. Elam.

WHAT WOULD YOU SAY....

What would you say if I told you
that Jesus was coming today?
Would you tell me you believe me,
or would you turn and walk away?

Would you smile and say,"At last He's here,
and finally I'm going home"?
Or would you turn and continue walking
down your same old road?

Would tears of joy come to your eyes
as you shout, "Thank you Lord!"
Or would you laugh and ridicule,
Because this is your world?

I'd like to know what you would do
when the world came to its end;
A man knows only his own heart,
are you alive or are you dead?

~Tracy Tammaro

NOT THEM

We love you God, we worship right,
we pray sincerely, fight the fight.
We open doors for those like us;
never failing to make a fuss
when someone new comes in the door.
They sure can help to give us more.
But wait, don't let that family in;
I know them well, they're steeped in sin.
And him, no he just wouldn't do.
I'm mad at him; I'm gonna sue.
And here, she isn't up to par;
she's too much trouble, won't go far.
I hate their children, hate that rake.
He's an idiot, she's a fake.
They make me angry, get me riled.
I cannot wait until the suit's been filed.
I love you, God; I love you well.
I never plan to go to hell.
I am right; and others wrong,
(different verses, same old song).
My hatred's surely justified.
It will not work, you know I've tried.
I can't accept them; never can.
But look at me, I'm sure your man.

~Richard L. Elam

IS TONIGHT THE NIGHT?

In the middle of the night I awoke hearing
   screams,
engulfed in much terror at what I'd just seen;
The pain dwelled inside me, so much hurt to see;
Lord, what can I do, was my moaning plea;
The whole world was in turmoil.....chaos if you
   will,
It's doom now ready, it's fate already sealed;
Blood flowed to the horses' bridles.... it ran red
   and deep,
The horror of the vision was worse than words
   can speak;
Who am I Lord to do anything?
Who would listen if such a message I should
   bring?
Only a servant with something needing to be said
of the doom that is coming...... lying just ahead;
So I put it in poem form.... an alert for this site,
For all who will listen.......tonight could be the
   night;
I open up my Bible reading Rev.14:20 in much
   fear,
and wonder if what I posted anyone would hear;
So many in the world don't believe the Lord's
   coming anymore
One of the signs that He's at the very door;
If you should read this poem ...... know the Lord
   will come when He may,
But it's the Christian's job to warn others
   everyday.

~*Gary Jenkins*
His Servant
2/23/98

POSITIONS OF THE HEART
Shall not God search this out?
for he knoweth the secrets of the heart.
Psalm 44:21

Many prayers are said which God will not accept,
For though a person kneels, a standing heart is kept;
The positions one may pray in are often different kinds,
What really matters to God is the condition of the minds;
God isn't looking at whether one kneels or stands,
He's not impressed a bit with a bow or folded hands;
The one thing that's important and God alone can see,
Is the position of the heart: is it how it ought to be?
One may lie in bed unable to utter a word,
Yet cries from the heart, God's already heard;
Only in their thoughts are some people able to pray,
Still with perfect hearing Jesus hears what they will say;
One can come to God, even while lying in their bed,
With a humble heart, without any fear or dread;
The one thing that's important and God alone can see,
Is the position of the heart: is it how it ought to be?

One thing is for certain when all is said and done:
Every knee shall bow at the coming of God's Son,
And every tongue confess that Jesus Christ is Lord,
A salutation given by all in one accord;
I believe some hearts will also be kneeling too,
And the ones that aren't won't be hidden from His view;
The ones that are standing, Almighty God will see,
And send them from His presence for all eternity.

~Gary Jenkins
The Servant

A SERVANT'S STATEMENT

The heart is so much like a butterfly's wings. It can show forth only the beauty (or light) the Lord has graced it with. Also like the butterfly's wing, once touched it is never the same again. Once the Lord touches a heart it will never again be the same. Should one turn from His grace, the heart will be left confused, parched without it's life-giving source....never again to be as it was. Praise God for grace and forgiveness, for without it there would be no hope. This is one servant who has been truly blessed by his God, the Lord Jesus Christ.

~Gary Jenkins
The Servant

NOW HE'S GONE

Your eyes are barely open,
the mist begins to set
loud noises you begin to shun,
still dew upon your eyes is wet.

You suddenly seem so all alone
while quietness fills the air.
There must be something going wrong,
but all you do is sit and stare.

It seems the time has come,
but where is there to go.
You may have had your pleasures,
but now they seem so long ago.

Recollections of the past
of what things could've been
Happiness you could've had
and hope are never again.

You go to find His letter
for some reassurance there,
but the love that He had offered you
remember, you didn't care.

You call to find a friend
and a loved one who was dear,
but it seems that they are missing
and chaos is everywhere.

Things start to fall in place
you recall that Trumpet blast!
It seemed to go on forever
yet, it's notes were clear and fast.

Everyone is in the streets
they're clamoring aimlessly,
what's that they're talking about?--
the dead Christians have left their sleep.

You stumble back inside
but find no solace there,
You finally realize that Christ returned
and you were left right here.

You hadn't prayed to God,
You hadn't read His word,
You hadn't even taken the time
to profess Him as your Lord.

Now He's Gone,
Jesus came back as He said
You missed the chance of heaven
and for all that Jesus bled.

You knew he died
just for your sin
but still you turned away
and didn't even try offer your heart to Him.

Now He's Gone,
If there were only hope
you "pray" you'll get another chance
but now, how do you cope?

You awaken at that moment
and realize just then
that God gave you a second chance
so kneeling down, your life you give to Him.

(Continued)

(Continued)

No more hesitations
You know now what you need
God's peace and love inside of you
and from sin to be freed.

Not only that
but so much more.
there's family and friends not saved
Now you go to witness, about your Lord.

The story is just this
don't wait 'til it's too late
Give you heart to Christ today
and help others to know the way.

The day could be "tomorrow",
or even be today.
Don't hesitate to call on Christ
"Tomorrow" may be too late.

    Dedicated to my big brothers:
    Randy and David Myers (Shank)

~Lisa M. Sackett

SELFLESSNESS VS. SELFISHNESS

There was a child,
small, innocent . . .
threatened.
And we dissatisfied
because we can't have more.
So little time to buy--
to give.
Giving is Christian,
isn't it?
Yet, there was that
infant, crying...
and parents
hoping for a real bed...
a sanitary place; not there.
Only several weeks left to shop.
I only have a few more
things to get.
I can't forget the party
we are having.
That, too, is important.
Fellowship--
that is Christian, too.
Please don't let the baby fuss.
I'll help. Let someone
help tonight.
I'll help tomorrow
afternoon . . .

~Richard L. Elam

WHAT IS JOY? ☺ JOY

Is joy an emotion
That's set off by smiles?
By all situations that
Make it last for awhile?

Is joy the emotion
That shows smiles and glee,
When all outside sources
Tell I'm happy with me?

If true joy's an emotion,
Then surely it fails
When everything changes
And then sadness prevails.

Then joy the emotion
Could not ever last,
For even in memories,
It's a thing of the past.

But true joy's a fountain
Flowing deep within,
That is bubbling forth
With forgiveness of sin.

Joy's the peaceful river,
Flowing from inside out;
It's the feeling you have
When there's not any doubt.

Joy's all in the knowing
That right's in the heart,
Then when sadness creeps in
Joy stays deep in the heart.

True joy will bring peace
And o'erflowing love waves,
And nothing, no nothing
Will ever drive it away!

-Patricia A. Behnken
May 15, 1998

♡

TRUE LOVE VS. EMOTIONS

Emotions
    Cause eyesight to fail,
    Tricks to prevail,
    Hurts to unveil,
    Truths to curtail,
    Peace to assail.

True Love causes
    Hatred to cease,
    Deceit to decrease,
    Truth to increase,
    Jealously to cease,
    Hearts full of peace.

~Patricia A. Behnken
June 15, 1998

CHRISTIAN LOVE???

I've heard about a Christian brother;
He sounds like such a great guy!
Above himself he always puts others;
When God leads, he never asks why.
He's coming to church to preach for us;
We'll all be treated tonight.
We'll all be coming just to be blessed;
I know he'll tell us just right.
I have been waiting so very long;
I'll hear him in church tonight.
But wait–I think I see something wrong–
No! My eyes can't believe the sight!
Why this man coming shouldn't be here,
His color is not like we are;
Why, who's the one who invited him here?
See, his skin color's not up to par.

There is a cute little girl, they say;
She always makes people smile;
She always has a nice word to say
When anyone's going through a trial;
She knows exactly how to pray,
And God always hears her prayers,
The word of God she reads every day,
And the scriptures she'll always share;
My friend is bringing her picture today,
So I can at least see her face;
I know I'll be taken with such a "sun ray,"
And her picture will brighten the place.
---My friend has been here to visit me
–Why did she play such a trick?
She brought "that girl" here to visit me,
And her color was not one we'd pick.

Some say that they are all good Christians:
Love their brethren as themselves,
Until they see another that's different,
Then they separate others from themselves;
Jesus allowed Himself to go tell
Where no one else had been:
He sat with a Samaritan at the well,
Till He saw deliverance from her sin;
Miriam and Aaron against Moses spoke,
Because of what they saw in his wife,
God with leprosy on Miriam smote;
Moses interceded for her very life;
God has made His word very clear:
Hate our brother, then love we bind;
Love sees the heart so very clear–
Love will make us all color blind.
(Human Race)

~Patricia A. Behnken
Feb. 17, 1998

TAKE THE TIME

I used to take the time
to just sit down and think,
and wonder if there was anyone
who could actually care for me.

Not knowing there was Someone
who would never leave my side,
who'd pick me up when I was down
and wipe the tears when I cried;

Who'd make my life worth living
when all hope seemed to be lost,
who'd calm my troubled heart,
stand by me at any cost.

Always being so close by
but never really there;
always knocking and waiting
to tell me that He cared;

Saying "Come, and let me dwell
within your heart today,
to give you joy, love and peace
and to live eternally.

I used to take the time
to just sit down and think
why anyone would care enough
to want to live in me.

But now Christ lives within
and I know He really cares,
for whatsoever state I'm in
He is always there.

And now I sit and think
of why it took so long,
to realize my only need
is to live for Christ alone.

~Lisa M. Sackett

GUIDANCE

DIECTION

✝

OR

ADMONITION

CHASING AFTER THE WIND

When Jesus asked me to follow in His steps I
 simply said
"I can make it all alone, I'll just go on ahead."

Then He said "I'll walk beside you," as He
 offered me His hand,
But I said "Really, I don't need you, on my
own I can stand."

Jesus said, "Then I will follow, to pick you
 up when you fall;
I'll be there to guide and comfort, if on Me
 you'll only call."

He wanted to be my Savior, He wanted to be
 my friend,
But I scorned His love and mercy as I chased
 after the wind.

After so many years, I finally called His
 precious name,
And just as He had promised, into my life He
 came.

He is forever faithful, always holding my
 hand,
He's there to lift me up and to be my closest
 friend.

There was no satisfaction in my life of sin,
It all was so elusive: that chasing after the
 wind.

~Doris Allen Davis
1998

TWINKLING OF AN EYE

In daily life we set our sights on things we don't know,
then tread down paths so many times we know shouldn't go;
In our youth we think for sure we'll live forevermore
and at life's end we'll ready ourselves to enter heaven's door;
But now is all the time we have that is truly ours,
and by His grace God has granted some of our desires;
So live your life as though this second is your last,
for no matter the allotted sum the end comes so fast;
Be ready at all time staying within God's grace,
for within the twinkling of an eye you may see His loving face.   ~*Gary Jenkins*
                        The Servant

EYES ON GOD

When life seems out of control,
Put your eyes on God.

When turmoil seems to take its toll,
Put your eyes on God.

When all your roads come up dead ends,
Put your eyes on God.

When you feel you need a friend,
Put your eyes on God.

With God, all things are possible.
               ~*Tracy Tammaro*

SEARCHING

We search for something tangible
to give our life it's will.
Unlike a glass that has no bottom ,
one can never fill.
You see there is a need one has,
to seek to justify.
Their ship among this life's harbor,
an anchor thus to tie.
I've drifted so amongst the waves,
no direction I have to steer.
It's almost as I've never struggled
or tried to even care.
You see it seems life's ocean huge
and vast beyond compare.
To sail against the current's fierce
seemed getting me nowhere.
But now I've gained experience,
a salty dog of sea.
I know my tillers true and strong,
thus takes me where to be.
I set my compass on the Lord
and fill my sails with faith.
For just beyond the horizon far,
I know that heaven waits.

~Kelley Lundborg

ON LETTING GO

Okay, I am ready and will once again take
   hold
with my determined actions, most
   meaningful style,
I can handle it, I know the ropes - thoughts
   so bold.
yes, grandly steer this ship of life for a while,
what mad pursuits, what journeys, what
   loves lost
so many good things I must and can do.
I am needed, it must be done, forget - the
   cost
I will prevail, I seek! if not me - why - then
   who?

Oh, my God what joy you bring!
You find me - remind kindly - I sing!
 --- You steady.
You hold in Your hands the rudder ready
You lift with infinite compassion, whole
To heal in Your light as You restore my soul.

~Jack Ellis

THE WINDING RIVER

What path are you walking
In your life from day to day?
Are you like the winding river
That takes the easy way?

If we look to ourselves for guidance
The path will lead us no where,
If we have a destination
Our Savior will take us there.

We need not fear the world
We have the power of God's might,
Unlike the winding river
He will be our guiding light.

If we'll follow in His path
We will not be lead astray,
We will forever be in His care
Our shepherd will lead the way.

God sees our every struggle
He knows the burdens that we bear,
He will answer our every need
If we will come to Him in prayer.

Never will He forsake us
In our failures or our fear,
As surely as we trust in Him
We can know that He is near.

We need not be like the river
That twists and winds it's way,
If we walk in the path that
God prepares for us each day.

What path are you walking
In your life from day to day?
Don't be like the winding river
That takes the easy way.

~*Doris Allen Davis*
1996

CHRISTIAN POLITICS

Jesus: Where were you when I was hungry?
Man: Out protesting, I was angry.
J: Where were you when I was hurt?
M: Helping spread a little dirt.
J: Where is food to feed the poor?
M: They looked like cheats; I shut the door.
J: Please, where are clothes and shelter, too?
M: I'm spending all my time for You.
Fighting for a Christian slate,
picketing, I can't be late . . .
J: Where were you when the roof caved in?
M: Ferreting out all public sin.
J: Just when I needed you the most,
you're running for some school board post.
Being a Christian isn't the same
as playing your political game.
You're so concerned with being pious,
protesting an anti-Christian bias;
Yet, you yourself refuse to see
how politics has made you be
the very thing you say you hate;
instead, you seem to celebrate
the victories and wish for more--
please, tell me how it was before,
when all you cared about was me;
you spread my love, helped people see
that this world is a passing life
filled with hatred, guilt, and strife.
Your job is to see it through,
help the poor, the homeless, too.
Let them see me through your touch,
this isn't hard, it won't take much.
Just be yourself, I'll be right there.
Can you do it? Do you dare?
Please fold up all the protest signs,
forget your crusade, just resign.
Allow our hearts to harmonize,
then you will see things with these eyes.
Where were you when darkness came?
Out playing some political game.

~*Richard L. Elam*

WOMAN'S FAULT

Dear Lord, that woman that you gave,
she tempted me, she knew I'd crave
anything she offered me--
she ate the fruit from off that tree,
then passed it on. I tried it, too,
but Eve should take the pain that's due.

Delilah is at fault, not me.
She used her charms, why can't you see?
She tricked me, till my heart lay bare,
then called her friends. They cut my hair.
I'm weaker now because of she.
That woman is to blame, not me.

It's not my fault, dear God, at all.
Ms. Bathsheba had the gall,
bathing there with flowing hair
in open sight--I know I'm right--
she tempted me.
Please, don't you see
that someone else should take the blame.
Women! They are all the same.
They take us down a primrose path,
then make us face the Master's wrath.

I really think it's quite unfair
that men should suffer and despair
just because a woman moved us,
led astray and tried to woo us.
Men are not at fault, no way.
Women are the ones to pay.

...What? You say this isn't so?
That we had choices, could say no?
Our sins are just as great as theirs;
that suffering must come in pairs?

Yes, we are guilty, we have sinned;
must turn our hearts, change, amend.
No more cast blame a woman's way.
Instead, admit our fault this day.

~Richard L. Elam

SOMETIMES THE ANSWER'S NO

I prayed a prayer dear Lord: I prayed it unto you,
then waited for a while to see what You would do;
There wasn't the slightest sign that You'd even heard,
As many questions arose causing me to doubt Your word;
My faith had been shaken as I gasped in disbelief,
distraught by no answer brought me so much grief;
My friends being aware prayed one and all,
For You to speak to me and I to hear Your call;
I was full of doubt blaming everything on fate,
Losing trust in the Lord put me in an awful state;
Words spoken in my mind were like a whisper far away,
as the Lord taught me a lesson I cherish still today...
My children's prayers are answered because I love them so,
I want what's best for them, and sometimes the answer's no.

~*Gary Jenkins*
The Servant

CAUTIONS

When you hear the cautions of the Lord,
Don't put up a block,
The Lord will never stop your way,
Just heed Him when He knocks.

He never screams in loud shrill voice,
He never blocks your way,
He whispers softly in your ear,
"Be careful, lest you stray."

If you listen when He speaks to you,
You'll be glad you heard His call,
You'll see how He's protected you
And kept you from a fall.

But if you choose to close your ear
And do as you desire,
It won't be long till you are trapped,
And the trial will seem as great fire.

The stumbling blocks will come your way,
It won't be easy to climb;
And everything will get much worse,
Cause you have set your mind.

At first it all may seem just right,
What you've chosen seems all good,
So you continue along that path,
Doing only as you would.

The longer you continue on
The harder it will be
Your eyes are closed unto the truth,
The lie you begin to believe.

Then suddenly you find you're in a trap,
It's hard to struggle out;
Your mind is filled with confusion,
And you begin to doubt.

It's hard to give up what you want,
Since having gone so long;
The things of God seem hard to grasp,
It's hard to sing a song.

But Jesus is gently calling still,
He has not forsaken you;
He's waiting for you to call on Him,
So He can rescue you.

Because of His word, He won't intrude
On your free will's delight,
But when you repent and ask His help,
He's there to help you fight.

The struggle will be much harder,
The tears will be much more
Than if you'd heeded His cautions
When He first knocked on your door.

So we need to learn our lessons
If we have erred in the past,
And when we hear His voice again,
We'll be sure to answer fast.

God in His great love and mercy
Is watching over us,
And all that He wants for our lives
Is in Him to put our trust.

God holds the key to peace, joy, love,
And happiness all life through,
So you need to heed His cautions
When He first speaks them to you.

~Patricia A. Behnken
April 17, 1998

PURSUED

Did you ever run from someone
and run and run in fear,
And then before escaping,
completely stop when they came near?
Giving up without a fight,
going back on your beliefs,
instead of running on ahead
and finding full relief?
Why would one insist on quitting
when the end is just in sight?
Why would one just throw in the towel
without a decent fight?
Our pursuer has no power
to take us at his will,
The only power he has is
if we turn over OUR will.
So the answer is keep running,
the end is coming in view.
And the only one victorious
at the finish line will be you.

~*Patricia A. Behnken*
July 7, 1998

FIGHT BACK

When the enemy comes to battle
And he shows you what you lack,
When he tries to steal your integrity,
The answer is to fight back.

Just stand your ground and defeat your foe
When he tries to knock you off track;
Just hold your head high and plant your feet,
Prepare yourself to fight back.

The Bible says the enemy flees,
He probably won't come back,
If you resist temptations he brings,
And you stand firm and fight back

Look your enemy straight in the eye,
Stand up tall and don't look back;
Keep your head held high, victorious,
And declare you're fighting back.

So when you are feeling discouraged,
And the dark clouds seem so black,
Your mountains will crumble to the sea,
Because you choose to fight back.

~Patricia A. Behnken
July 27, 1998

RELEASED

My Jesus I love Thee, I know Thou are mine
When I fall on my face You care
But when I take wings and rise to the sky,
My Jesus You're the one who is there.

Your love seems to shine so much brighter
When down in the valley I've trod
In trials so deep, I shouldn't have been
Had I just kept my eyes upon God.

Yet, You will not fail me though I've failed You
You're there waiting open-armed for me,
And You will refresh me and renew my strength
And restore all that was taken from me.
                –AMEN

Our God is truly a jealous God
And requires that nothing be above Him
If we are not careful of the pathway we take
We find others to put above Him.

We begin to depend on the strength of man
Instead of depending on God,
A human can only lead in darkness
For he sees not the true light as God.

As far as I know there is not a person
Who wishes to take God's part
The stress of that office is too much to bear
And the burdens weigh heavy on the heart.

It is never fair to lay all our cares
Upon the heart of another
The burdens belong only to God
And not in the hands of our brother.

Don't get me wrong....our burdens we share
And help to bring others along
But we can't take advantage of our brothers'
   caring
Or we'll wind up stealing their song.

So we must learn to depend on God
He's there watching over us all. ...
And He will supply today all our needs
Our desires, and joys when we call.

So trust in God and only Him
Cast all your burdens on the Lord
And release your brother from the ties that
   bind
And break bands with God's Holy Sword.

And friendships will then be greater
Than they've ever been in the past
For love that comes with choices
Brings an enduring friendship that lasts.

~Patricia A. Behnken
April 29, 1998

THE LILY

As you stand in the lily field and you pick one, it seems like it says, "Child, don't turn loose of the Root of David because I'm coming soon." You look at the lily, and you know it could be you; because when you pull it away from the rest, you know it'll die. And that's the way we are: Pulled away from the Spirit, we die-- like the lily - no roots....and without roots - no life. But if we stay rooted in the Lord, we shall have life everlasting. *"...and because they had no root, they withered away."*
--Matthew 13:6

~Margaret A. Burchfield

THE VALLEY

I was going through a valley; it was dark and cold, and I felt all alone.
I walked where I always walked, but things were not the same, because I was looking through natural eyes.
Halfway through the valley, God spoke and said, "Child, you must walk this way, but you are not alone. Take time to look at the beauty in the valley; I am in the beauty of the flowers and I am in the streams. In the valley, My Spirit brings peace."

~Margaret A. Burchfield

CHRISTIAN ATTRIBUTES RESPONSIBILITIES

✝

OR OBLIGATIONS

EVERY TIME A SOUL IS SAVED

Every time a soul is saved
There's one less life to waste,
Every time a soul is saved
The world becomes a better place.

Every time a soul is saved
And one makes that fateful choice,
For just that one that is saved
All the angels in heaven rejoice.

We strive to find the answers
To life's troubles and it's strife,
We try by all ways and means
To have a better life.

We look to ourselves to resolve
Our problems great and small,
We expect the world to provide
A solution for one and all.

But all the time is wasted
Seeking help where there is none,
For the answer to every problem
Can come only from Christ the Son.

He is there to bear our burdens
And to calm all our fears,
He will take care of our needs
He will wipe away our tears.

We are our brother's keeper
We must each do our part,
To spread the word of God's love
And how He lives in our heart.

Reach out to a friend or stranger
Who knows not the Lord today,
Tell of His goodness and mercy
That He is the light and only way.

~Doris Allen Davis
1996

LET ME BRING YOUR MESSAGE

Let me be Your hope to others
As You are hope to me,
Let me reach out to a stranger,
Let me help someone in need.

Let me seek out the ones
Whose grief is hard to bear,
I'll tell them they are not alone
That You will always be there.

Let me comfort someone
Who is hurting today,
Let me bring them reassurance,
You're their help and mainstay.

Let me bring those together
Who have drifted apart,
Let me help them realize
That You live in their heart.

Let me find a doorstep
Of someone in distress,
I will share the good news
Of how their life You will bless.

Let me be a good friend
To those in need of one,
I will tell how You love them
And of all that You have done.

Let me find those who are lost
Or who have wandered astray,
I will tell them of the light
That will always guide their way.

Let me bring Your message
As it was brought to me,
Let us all be together
With You, in love, eternally.

~*Doris Allen Davis*
1996

NOTHING TO DO

An old soul, a sad soul, a dying soul,
lost and undone,
without anyone
to show him the way.
Where are the workers? The harvest is ripe,
the fruit is fat,
where is that
sickle to reap the crop?
There's nothing to do but sit on the pew
and warm our hearts
beside the hearth
of the local neighborhood church.
Tickle our ears and amuse our thought,
as we go each day
in our own way,
to carry our cross.
Our cross is heavy, too hard to bear,
because our brother
turns to another
and speaks against us.
Too much to worry and be concerned about
to think of the soul
without a goal
and to offer him Christ.
A dying soul, harvest in sight,
we close our eyes
and let him die,
because there's nothing to do.

~*Patricia A. Behnken*
June, 1993

SOLDIERS OF CHRIST

We're soldiers in the army of Christ,
Souls are dying,
Don't stop trying
to win them to Christ.
Souls wandering without any hope,
lost in the dark
with only a spark
from the light we reflect from God.
Souls reaching from enveloping darkness
for the Word
they've never heard,
of Christ's salvation so free.
Workers are the chosen few
to seek out souls,
making them whole
through the cleansing blood of the Lamb.
Taking to us the armor, of God,
Spirit wrestling
Satan's hassling,
No match is he against God.
Trials do come, hard and sore,
We carry the cross,
not counting the cost,
to rescue the perishing, our goal.
Awaiting the comforting words of our Lord:
"Welcome here,
My servants dear,
Enter ye into thy rest."

~*Patricia A. Behnken*
June, 1993

A CHILD LOST

I looked into this child's eyes,
which should be full of dreams;
Sparkling like the stars in the sky,
innocent they should seem;

Dancing when the child smiles,
happiness should overflow;
But, what I saw will haunt me now,
I saw a lonely, lost, empty soul.

Lord, this is just a baby,
barely even grown;
He should be living a child's life,
instead, he's afraid and alone.

There are many more just like him,
not knowing where to go,
and yet so many people,
just don't know what to do.

Lord, please watch over them,
guide their every step;
Let them feel Your presence,
for they feel there's nothing left.

~Tracy Tammaro

LITTLE VOICES

I'll pray for you, little voices say,
Please remember to pray for me,
So I can be good, so I can please God,
So I can be what He wants me to be.

I'll pray for you, little voices say,
Please be there to show me the way;
Don't let us down in the way you live,
Please show us the straight, narrow way.

I'll pray for you, little voices say,
That you can be satisfied
That you've led us the way that we should
    go
To grow up proven and tried.

I'll pray for you, little voices say;
Lets not be deaf to their silent cries,
Their excitement and longing to learn God's
    Word,
Little voices that speak with their eyes.

Who are the little voices that we hear plead?
They're preachers and teachers, missionaries,
    more
That tomorrow will spread God's Word ever
    far,
But today we're the ones to open the door.

~Patricia A. Behnken
1973

PRAYER OF A TEACHER

The life of a child–so precious, so dear!
Great treasures of happiness to those who are near.
A child, so tender, You hold close to Thy heart,
And blessings of love to each You impart.
The gift of a child for a teacher to show
All the ways to Thy glory is an honor to know.
This life Thou hast placed in our hands so weak
Has caused us to pray and Thy will to seek.
For Thou knowest the ones who will cause Them to learn,
So that they may see Heaven and eternal life earn.
God grant me the wisdom to teach every one
To lift up their hearts to receive Thine own Son.
And treasures on high Thou hast promised us all–
To each who is willing to heed Thy great call.
Oh thank You, dear Jesus, to Thee God above
For giving me children to teach of Thy love.

~Patricia A. Behnken

IF I COULD

If I could make a difference
in the way a day turns out,
I'd make them happy as I could,
this done without a doubt;
I'd gather all the sunbeams bright
and shine them down on you,
But leave enough of rain you see
to grow the flowers too;
A careful mix of certain things
to make your life be good,
So you would know I cared for you
as certain loved ones would;
Someday maybe, it'll come to pass,
an angel I'll become,
And God will say "why don't you watch,
over this special one."
Imagine joy, hardly contained,
to know that I can give
All the things to make you happy
in the life you live.

—*Kelley Lunborg*

THEY DON'T KNOW ME

My life's so strange, they look around yet
   they still don't see
the love , the pain, even the hurt in me.
They look, criticize, and turn away,
   though if they don't look inside of me they
   can't really say.
They say what they will
even saying the unknown--
that's all I am, because that's all I've shown..
They don't care to stop and listen, nobody
   hears my soft sad cries;
they say they've looked but now they're off
   spreading those nasty lies.
What do they know?
What would they know?
I wish they would just stop and look at the
   true me inside.   ~*Lana St. John*

PONDERING

My heart wonders at all the sad and lonely
   hearts–
The hurt, rejected and disabled hearts
who cry for someone,
Someone to care and someone to share,
Someone to lend a shoulder,
Someone to help carry the burdens and the
   pain;
The night is empty and still–oh so dark;
Lord, help the lonely and desolate,
Help them to find hope,
Help them to find help, friendship and caring;
Lead us to the ones we can help,
To help them find a caring hand,
To help the darkness turn to light
And the empty heart to be filled with hope–
Sadness to laughter, mourning to joy.
Help them to find the peace of
the Christ Child, their reason for living
        ~*Patricia A. Behnken* Dec. 1993

YE ARE THE LIGHT OF THE WORLD

Be full of smiles instead of sad,
Let everyone see you can be glad:
Let laughter ring and not complain,
Show them not a heart filled with rain.

Be thankful to God and full of praise,
Let them see Christ fills your days;
Instead of bitterness and full of doubt,
Have faith and trust and be ready to shout.

Show victory in Christ when they draw near,
Not defeat from the devil and tremble with
 fear;
Let them see Jesus, the Priceless Pearl,
Show compassion and love,
Ye are the light of the world.

~Patricia A. Behnken
November 17, 1989

NO ONE TO CARE

In my trembling hand
I held the tear-stained note,
As I read the final words
That she ever wrote:

"I have no reason for living
My life I cannot bear,
There is no one to love me
There is no one to care."

She was only sixteen,
With her life yet to live,
She asked so very little
And had so much to give.

All were saddened by her death,
For no one was aware
Of her feeling of loneliness
Or of her deep despair.

Just as we cannot see
Within the heart of another,
Neither can someone know
How we feel toward the other.

Let us not take for granted
That our love is readily known,
But by our every word and deed
Let God's love through us be shown.

It takes so very little time,
A pleasant smile, a kind word,
A loving expression of
God's caring and concern.

Perhaps we will never know
That what we've done or said
Could prevent another's writing
The saddest words I ever read:

"I have no reason for living
My life I cannot bear,
There is no one to love me
There is no one to care."

~Doris Allen Davis
1996

HIS HAND EXTENDED

You may not see your Lord nearby,
But you can see my smiling face;
You may not feel His tender touch,
But my hand o'er your brow you can trace.

Your ear may not hear His gentle voice,
But my song may comfort your soul;
His healing power you may long to feel,
And we pray together that He make you
   whole.

Lord, let us be Your hand extended–
To show Your love, mercy and grace;
Though others may not see through natural
   eyes,
Let us be a reflection of Your lovely face.

~Patricia A. Behnken
October 20, 1994

SILVERED HALOS

When looking at someone older, one generally thinks of a father figure, and it should, but doesn't always, bring to mind respect.

Myself, I think of a quote made by some wise person who said, "Anyone can be a father, but to truly be a daddy one has to be special." This is the way I look at the elders in our church. Elder doesn't mean older: older means God has granted someone long life. Elder means it has been a righteous one. Does that mean perfect? No, not by any stretch of the imagination. However, it does mean Spirit led where the fruits of the Spirit will be seen. Elders, when led by the Holy Spirit, are the true leaders of any church because being tried strengthens one's faith, brings appreciation, and so often humbles one's heart with which God looks upon. They teach us the truths of standing strong, of commitment, and that love is not a word but an action. Our elders are more than just pillars in the church: they are Spirit filled temples. They give and have given unselfishly of their time, never faltering in faith. Always teaching, they've dedicated their children and homes. Showing continually the directions of their hearts, they are light to illuminate the way in darkness and flames of warmth in the cold--a task that is impossible except for lives lived for Jesus. Therein lies the meaning of a true elder, one who has aged, knowing Jesus is the solid rock, standing on that, and teaching all the younger. In our Church I look at the elders, as many others do, and finding we have truly been blessed with the ones in our midst. Those are not grayed hairs that I see: instead they are beautiful silver halos.

~*Gary Jenkins*
The servant

FAMILIES

☦

AND

FRIENDSHIP

Chapter Dedication

I am dedicating this chapter to Jeremiah Shank for the simple reason that I made a big error in my book "Pathways Of My Journey" that involved him. On page 48 I had a picture of Jeremy's entire family printed in the book. When typing in their names, I looked at Jeremy's younger picture and forgot it was him and temporarily thought that it was Nathan Howell, Jeremy's little nephew. Therefore, I typed in the wrong name under the picture and didn't acknowledge Jeremy as himself. I didn't find my error until the book was already completed and it was too late.

    I have known Jeremy all his life and love him very much. I've already asked his forgiveness and he has forgiven me. I hope that this dedication makes up a little bit for the error I made. The following poem also is dedicated to Jeremy as well.

FORGIVENESS

Forgiveness is kind,
Forgiveness is good;
We all make mistakes
We'd avoid if we could.
So forgiving another
In his unplanned error
May help someone else
To forgive us tomorrow.

~*Patricia A. Behnken*

Jeremiah Shank

MY TEACHER GRACE HART

In memory I've kept the thoughts of one~
a teacher to me so dear;
Such an impact she had on directing my path,
I was privileged as her student one year.

The year was filled with exciting things:
poetry, short stories, the rest;
Geography was interesting, game time was too,
but of course, there were also the tests!

In my memory I've kept the special time
that my teacher visited for lunch;
What we ate doesn't matter and slips my mind,
but I know I was proud "a whole bunch"!

If I could go back to change part of my life,
I know I'd have that year remain;
For the year I was taught by our precious Grace
Hart
was nothing for me but great gain.

Yesterdays memories seem almost like dreams,
but since then our paths crossed again;
Yesterday holds memories of a teacher so grand,
but in my heart now I've found a good friend.

~*Patricia A. Behnken*

I wrote this poem in honor of my sixth grade teacher
who was the one who sparked the interest in me for
poetry and writing. All during the year she had us
memorize and recite poetry, and I learned to love it.
I am thankful to her that she was such a wonderful
teacher to me and many other students during her
teaching career. May the Lord bless her abundantly,
even as she has blessed us all!

DEDICATION FOR HE'S NOT HURTING ANYMORE

I wrote "He's Not Hurting Anymore" for a dear friend of mine, James Schneider. I knew him as Jim. Jim died after suffering from cancer a couple years. So when I received the phone call that he had passed away, my first thoughts were "He's not hurting anymore."

I loved and respected this man as much or more than anyone I have ever met. He was a fine Christian. He taught the young adults' class in our church. My two youngest girls were in his Sunday school class. They admired and respected this man with all their hearts, often telling me how much. I didn't look up Jim's birth or death, because his real birth was when he was born again, and his death will never really be; he had the promises of eternal life.

Since love lasts forever and sweet memories are a precious jewel, Jim left all who knew him with a treasure cherished more than gold.

~*Gary Jenkins*
The Servant

HE'S NOT HURTING ANYMORE

The phone rang with news we'd been expecting today,
the sad news of our friend's passing away.
For awhile there was only silence, words were hard to find,
As thoughts of my dear friend entirely filled my mind.
When I spoke, breaking the silences of before,
The only words I could think of were:
he's not hurting anymore.

No he's not hurting anymore, all his pain's been replaced
with the happiness he feels, for all his hurt's been erased.
Now he walks with Jesus in the promised land,
things he didn't know, he clearly understands.
Only our Lord Jesus knows all He has in store,
But there's one thing for certain,
he's not hurting anymore.

We'll all get together in a place his wife will choose,
talking of our dear friend whom we all had to lose;
Each one wishing what was hadn't been
and that we could all see him at least once again.
But he's with our Lord Jesus, where he'll be forevermore;
The Lord has wiped away all his tears,
No, Jim's not hurting anymore.
        Rev. 21:4

~*Gary Jenkins*
The Servant

CIRCLE OF LOVE

The years have sent us every one
to find our separate ways,
yet love has always brought us back
no matter where we've strayed.

My heart is filled with happiness
as I gaze upon each face.
I am reminded of the past,
some other time, some other place.

Years have passed and we have grown,
our daily lives no longer shared,
yet through each joy and tragedy
for one another we have cared.

Some we loved have passed away,
and in our hearts are greatly missed,
yet their spirits remain near and dear,
for by their presence we were blessed.

Should ever we feel lost and alone,
the burden we carry too heavy to bear,
all we need do is reach out our hand
and someone we love will be there.

Our circle of love can never be broken
no matter how far we wander or roam,
the love that we share spans time and space,
a continuous link to family and home.

~*Donna M. Givens*

THE LITTLE CHURCH

It was just a little church
But it was filled with love,
All the congregation
Were strengthened from above.

Though they were few in number,
Those who came were always blessed
By God's word and His songs
On their day of rest.

When strangers came to visit,
They could always feel
The love and joy in God's house
And know that it was real.

Every time a soul was saved
There in the little church,
All the people would rejoice
Praising God, who'd done so much.

They laughed and cried together,
Joys and burdens they did share
Together in the little church,
For God was with them there.

They all were very special,
They loved each other, you see,
For that's the way it is
When you're part of God's family.

For God's mercy and His grace
I thank Him, oh, so much,
For my life has been changed
Since I found that little church.

~Doris Allen Davis
1996

LIKE-KIND CHRISTIAN FRIENDS
Faithful are the wounds of a friend;
but the kisses of an enemy are *deceitful.*
Proverbs 27:6

Sometimes God in His infinite wisdom
Sends people into our lives;
It's easy to see another's faults,
But our own are covered sometimes with pride.

But when we see friends and hear their words
That mirror weaknesses of our own,
Then truth will reveal we are as they are
And answers to our own faults can be known.

Their friendships can surely make us grow
If we use all that's revealed to us,
Taking all we've discovered as instruction,
Using the reflection of ourselves to be blessed.

~*Patricia A. Behnken*
April 10, 1998

DISTANCE

...The Lord watch between me and thee,
when we are absent one from another.
Genesis 31:49b

As I drive, I look ahead and see the clouds before me as white puffy balls of cotton,
the blue sky shining brightly in the sun--
and I feel good.
Distance is no longer, as I feel God watching over us:
even as a child would peer into a doll house,
seeing every room, every doll, every piece of furniture.
Nothing can move or even blink an eye without His knowing it.
Looking at the sky, I realize that,
though the weather may be different there,
it is the same atmospheric covering surrounding you
as surrounds me.
I realize that you are alive and living this day through,
even as I am--
and it feels good to know my friend is living in the
same world--
I feel connected--and distance is no more.
> Lord, watch over my friend each day,
> thank you for this peace I feel within,
> and tell my friend to whisper a prayer for me,
> looking up at the starry sky tonight........Amen

~Patricia A. Behnken
April 21, 1998

A BASKET OF GIFTS

We have not given you a gift, you said,
Ah, yes, but you have my dearest friends--
You've given me a smile when I was down,
When I was lonely, you stayed around;
You didn't forsake me when I felt lost,
You gave me your time, not counting the cost;
When I felt confused and unable to think,
Your help from God's Word was refreshing drink;
And just letting me speak all the thoughts of my heart,
Caused peace to come and fears to depart;
And when there seemed too much to do,
Without a thought, you came to the rescue
You jumped right in with pure physical labor,
You forgot about you and just thought of your neighbor;
Your kindnesses are greater than I can express,
You are all so special and have given your best;
So you see my friends, I have a basket of gifts,
So great and costly and so heavy to lift;
With the natural eye, you're unable to see--
I thank you for best gifts you've give to me.

~*Patricia A. Behnken*
December 9, 1989

A MEMORIAL TO OUR BROTHER
Dedicated in memory of Jack Pyle
1929--1995

Jack, we love your smiling face,
Especially when we sing "Amazing Grace."
Your greatest testimony, though to some
  would be hard,
Was when you buried the TV in your back
  yard.

You talked of how God changed your ways:
He turned your angers into praise,
He turned your darkness into light
And made your countenance beaming bright.

The first to stand and then begin
To give God glory and worship Him–
The Spirit of God would soon then draw,
To our feet we'd stand, the rest of us all.

Your leadership and kindness great:
Some of your most wonderful traits,
Your humble spirit from your new birth
Are surety that you shall inherit the earth.

Because of you, we've all been touched,
And we all love you so very much;
We see your fist clenched, showing power of
  God
And hear your words: "We serve a mighty
  God!"

~*Patricia A. Behnken*
January 25, 1995

THE APPLE OF FRIENDSHIP

A man that hath *friends*
must shew himself friendly: . .
Proverbs 18:24a

The trip was long and tiresome too,
And I felt I'd never get there,
The many stops brought people new,
Everyone going somewhere;
People got on and people got off,
Most we'd never see again,
But from one stop came a person unknown,
Yet soon to be a friend;
As with some others that before her had come,
We began to talk and learn
Something about each other to share
That we had in common concerns;
We talked about our love of the Lord,
Some testimonies we shared,
A friendship began on a bus ride so long,
But the time... neither cared;
The couple hours our visit continued
Flew by as a fleeting sigh,
And before we were ready our visit had ended,
And it was time to say goodbye;
An apple she gave me during our ride,
A token of friendship that day;
As I accepted her gift, I accepted a friend,
Though memories of the trip would fade;
Today I can say I hardly recall
All the things that we said on our trip,
But the apple she gave I remember so clear
Was the start of our long friendship.

-Patricia A. Behnken
1/8/98
In honor of my friend,
Marianne Thomas

JOY IN THE MORNING

Jesus, Dear Lord,
Please take care of my friend,
Please let him be all right;
Restore to him Your peace,
Bring him safely through the night.

As the storm rushes in its rage,
And it's hard to hold on tight,
Speak Your word peace be still--
Bring him safely through the night.

When the waves come crashing o'er,
And the coldness begins to bite,
Reach Your hand and bid him come,
Bring him safely through the night.

When the darkness hovers in,
And it's 'most impossible to fight,
Let Your light come shining through;
Bring him safely through the night.

Let him rest in Your love divine
and be encouraged with morning's light;
As new day begins to dawn, he'll know
he's made it safely through the night.

For the morning will bring him new hope,
And new strengths shall arise upright,
His joyful praises will bubble forth, knowing
You've kept him safe throughout the night.
 --Amen
~*Patricia A. Behnken*
April, 1998

GRANDMA
Dedicated in memory of
Johanna Boehner Kidder, 1891-1980
Grandmother of Susan Lloyd, Patricia Behnken,
Judith Vance, Sarah Walton, and Kathy Divilleri

She was the most real person I've ever known. I never heard her say an unkind word to anyone or about anyone as long as I knew her.

My first memories of Grandma are of someone who was always there, always loving, always laughing and happy, always making me feel very special. I never remember seeing her rest. She was always doing something–usually for someone else.

She was very feminine, very modest, but yet I remember Grandpa proudly talking about the times she put on a pair of trousers and climbed up to shingle the roof or picked cotton in the fields. She loved life and enjoyed it to the fullest.

She was always stubborn and hard-headed when it came to her own physical limitations. More often than not, she simply refused to be ill. Her independence was very important to her.

During this last year of her life, she never gave up. She fought every day, determined to get out of bed–to walk again–to go home. She died as she lived–strong in mind if not in body. Now that she has ceased breathing, she still lives for us and for everyone who has ever known her. The lessons she taught by the way she lived her life have touched us all.

And, even now, she has won again–this stubborn, determined, wonderful lady! She finally found her way home and back to Grandpa and her family. If you listen hard enough, you can almost hear her laughing once again in joy. God bless her. We loved her very much.

~Susan L. Bayless Lloyd
February 13, 1980

Susan was writing this the evening Grandma died, not knowing that it was right before she went on to be with her Lord.

SHE WAS NEVER ALONE

I often think of Grandma
And all she meant to me,
I remember her endless love
For her Lord and family.

In the last years of her life
After the Lord took Grandpa home,
She could neither walk nor see,
But never was she alone.

When I would visit Grandma
I would quietly call her name,
She would brighten with a smile
And say, "I'm so glad you came."

She would talk about the past:
What she and Grandpa used to do,
She'd tell me all the stories
I had forgotten or never knew.

I would hold her wrinkled hand
And brush her snow-white hair,
I'd tell her how I loved her,
How much I would always care.

Each time before I left her
One thing she would always do,
In her weak, but still-sweet voice
She'd sing "God Will Take Care of You."

And take care of her, He did,
No, she was never alone,
He was there beside her
"Til He called her to come home.

~Doris Allen Davis
1996

DELICIOUS!
Dedicated to my grandchildren
Jessica, Joshua and Bethany Malone

"Being a grandmother is delicious!"
someone once said to me;
I had no grandchildren of my own,
so she said, "Just wait and see."

So when the first one was on her way,
I thought I was prepared,
but the joy I felt when I saw her
to nothing could be compared.

'Twas like again seeing my own child,
so much like her mommy,
like having my baby back again;
Was just like cotton candy!

I thank the Lord for sending them all,
God gave each His special touch;
I love all three in their special ways,
God has blessed me, oh so much!

~Patricia A. Behnken
July 13, 1998

MOTHER
Dedicated to Mary Bayless

Mother, what would I ever do without you,
As long as I recall, you've been there for me;
You've never waited till I called to you,
But you've watched and known what I need.

You encouraged me in all that I did,
You were gentle and kind, when I was small,
And watched over me and picked me up
Every time that you saw me fall.

I was sick and took lots of your time,
But I don't remember your first complaint
You always seemed to have the remedy
And your loving touch was like a saint.

You were the one who taught me to pray
And started my mind on God to think
And I prayed each night for Him to keep us
And with that prayer, off to sleep I'd sink.

When I grew older and more sickness came
You were so faithful and ever near
Your help you gave almost everyday
Your love was so precious and dear.

Today as I am older, you're still my friend
We share more than we did before
Since Jesus has come into your heart
Our fellowship has become more and more.

And then someday we have the hope
That eternity we'll together be
And together we'll share the love of God
When His blessed face we see.

If there's a reward just for good mothers,
I know that reward will be yours
For you have been faithful to all your children
And you'll surely enter Heaven's doors.

Patricia A. Bayless Behnken
May, 1998

A MOTHER'S LOVE

We cannot count our many gifts
But we know that we've been blessed,
For each of us God 'specially chose
One mother from all the rest.

To her, God gave a special sight
To see the beauty from within,
That makes each child unique indeed
Unlike any other child has been.

With the loving touch of her hand
She can dry the wettest tears,
And with her quiet reassurance
She can calm her children's fears.

She has a special healing power
Unlike that of any other,
When nothing else helps the hurt
God gives us the touch of a mother.

God bestowed upon the mothers
Lots of tender, loving care
And extra kisses, smiles and hugs,
So they'd have more to share.

And God chose the very biggest hearts
From all His vast array
To give to mothers everywhere,
For He knew there would come a day

When their hearts would just overflow
With all the love deep inside
That sweet, embracing love of a child
That only a mother can provide.

~*Doris Allen Davis*
1997

MEMORIES OF MOM

I have many fond memories of mom,
memories that allow me to grab hold
of life as it should be.
Tonight I see
Mom comfortingly -
bringing the cool, asked for,
glass of milk,
sipping very slowly,
wanting the glass never empty,
looking to her smiling face,
receiving her blessing,
snuggling deep down,
reassured into my covers;
Oh, to be able to ask one more time,
"Mom, please leave the light on."
~*Jack Ellis*

A FRIEND

I have a friend so dear to me
who listens when I cry,
Someone who shares the world with me,
though at times I don't know why.

She's always there to comfort me,
whenever, day or night;
She knows just what to do and say
to make it all seem right.

Although I may not show it enough,
I appreciate all she's done;
Because without her in my life,
the battles, I'd never have won.

I want to say how much I care,
my love will never end;
For she is the one who gave me life,
I'm blessed that she's my friend
~*Tracy Tammaro*

JESUS IS HERE FOR AUNT BETTY

She's writing a will, withdrawing her
    account,
leaving her possessions for her sinner loved
    ones;
She's paying her debts and talking about
when that day comes and the angels all
    shout.

Arise He has come, arise each and everyone,
Your master is here, too late for one more
    prayer.

Like an angel she seems to me, has a light
    that shines
so bright, spreading her golden wings,
Preparing for a great and wonderful flight.

Arise He has come, arise each and everyone
The Master is here, all judgement must be
    fair.

I know she has that power to meet Him in
    the air
and confess that she has loved Him,
And followed Him everywhere.

And on that day that Jesus appears
Heaven is ready and Satan is there,
She'll bow down humbly, turn to her loved
    ones,
cry out softly, her eyes full of tears,
You would not listen, I tried to warn you,
My family I love you, but Jesus is here.

Written for my Aunt BettyBarnett
~*Nancy Blythe* 1981
Deceased 1998

DADDY

Sometimes our father, 'till we're grown
we do not realize
the blessing that he was to us
above all other guys!

He was there providing for us
and gone a lot of times,
working hard a lot of hours
to make our lives just fine.

He taught us that we shouldn't fear
the storms that rage outside,
but keep a peace within our hearts
and never run to hide.

He taught us to do well in school,
our very best to do,
so that when we became grown up
our best we'd continue.

He taught us to care for others;
He taught us the golden rule,
to do unto others as you'd
have them do unto you.

So now thinking of our father
and all the good in him,
we can put behind all hard times
and be thankful for him.

God will grant us peace of mind and
good memories for us,
and knowing a special father,
God really gave to us.

~*Patricia A. Bayless Behnken*
July 22, 1998

MY FIRST PARADE
Dedicated to my father, James Bayless

My first parade my daddy was there
to carry me in the air,
lifting me up so I could see
the colorful parade go by;
Marchers and streamers
and batons twirling by,
horses and wagons and clowns
with smiles and frowns,
laughter and music
and squealings of glee,
as the drums and the trumpets
passed by with celebration;
I held close to my daddy,
my heart pounded with joy,
A sight and sound memory to be always
embedded in my mind;
Now the sounds of parades that ever pass by,
or the music of a carrousel
forever will spark the memory
of that eventful night–
when my daddy took me to a parade.

~*Patricia A. Bayless Behnken*

The following poem was submitted by Kimberly L. Mikesell in fun and loving tribute to her father Gene Hollingsworth for his first poem. **(eye twinkles) ☺

THE BALL GAME
Rain
No game
~*Gene Hollingsworth*

MY DAUGHTER MY FRIEND
Dedicated to Renee Malone

When I need a friend to talk to
When I need a friend so true
I know that you will listen
And I can talk to you.

When I need someone to love me
When I need someone to care
I know that you will love me
And my devotions you will share.

When I need a heart to open
And I need to feel a part
I know you understand me
And share what's in my heart.

You'll always be my "valentine"
If it means I love you true
And want to be here for you,
For my daughter I love you.

~*Patricia A. Behnken*
February 14, 1998

A MOTHER'S PRAYER

Dear Lord let her always
be healthy and strong.
Fill her heart with joy,
and her voice with song.
Be always beside her
to show her the way.
Love and protect her
throughout all of her days.
Let her show mercy
and treat others with care.
Let her finest attire
be the smile that she wears.
Let her find beauty
in all that she sees.
Fill her with hope
in her times of need.
Give her patience and courage
for what lies ahead.
A place of shelter
and her daily bread.
The wisdom to choose
right over wrong.
The strength to lead,
not just follow along.
Let her touch be gentle
and her words be kind.
Bless her with fairness
and an open mind.
Let grace and beauty
fill her soul,
and guide her steps
wherever she goes.

~Donna M. Givens

A PARENT'S PRAYER

The day you were born I held you so near,
praying my first prayer for you, oh my dear,
I didn't ask for wealth of a tangible kind,
instead that you'd have riches of the mind;
I prayed as I touched your every part,
for your health with all of my heart,
I prayed for wisdom with all of my might,
that I may know how to teach what is right;
Knowing when to discipline the way I
   should,
giving guidance in what is right and good,.
Not to strike in anger with hurting blows,
but to give you love that always shows;
Then last but so very far from least,
I prayed the Lord to give you lasting peace,
That you'd live for Jesus while upon this
   earth;
This was my special prayer, on the day of
your birth.

~*Gary Jenkins*
The Servant
6/22/97

FOR OUR SAKES

My little girl came to me with tears in her eyes,
asking me a question that cause me to sigh;
A friend's angry words had caused her some doubt
of being a mistake, so she came to find out;
I sat her on my knee then kissed her on the cheek,
trying not to cry when I began to speak,
" Once there was a couple so much in love
they were given a blessing sent from up above;
They weren't asked any questions or given any test,
Yet received a gift far better than a tongue could request;
She had just enough hair for her mom to comb,
a cute little nose looking like dad's very own;
She was so sweet and tiny that when they held her close,
they knew they'd been blessed far more than most.
No they had not planned her, but love is never planned,
It's a gift of the Lord's from His very own hand;
He's the one who knows what's best for our lives
and gives just the right child to men and their wives;
I believe when He does it, He does it with a smile,
as He teaches of Himself through the eyes of a child.
No my darling daughter dear, you are far from a mistake,
The Lord gave you to us for your mom's and my sake;
And if we could have chosen from all the children in this world,
There's no way we would have chosen any other boy or girl."

~*Gary Jenkins*
The Servant

SUSAN
MY SISTER, MY SECOND MOTHER,
MY TEACHER, MY FRIEND

In growing up, I always knew
My sister would be near,
In everything both bad and good,
I knew she'd always hear.

Sunday mornings, while others slept,
To her room I'd quietly go,
We'd sit upon her bed and share
'Til things in her heart I'd know.

My sister was like a mother too,
And she was always dear,
She was always watching over us
And all our problems hear.

–Toothbrushes clean and all beds made,
for arguing made no allowance,
Then little charts she made for us
And graded us on our performance.

Friday nights came and oh what glee!
–pizza, chips and song!
What fun we had singing "Wayward Wind"
Seemed that nothing could go wrong.

When special times came, she planned a play
Perform for our parents, we did;
At Christmas time I played a grandma,
Reading Bible stories to grandkids.

During homework time, I was the ear
To hear Latin words being learned,
And Latin it was that I did pick
When choosing a class, it was my turn.

In all our growing-up childhood years,
Teaching us manners, respect and fun,
It was Susan who was always there,
And for help, to her we would run.

The day she said she was going to marry
And that she'd be going away,
We cried so sad, but still she was
A pretty bride on her wedding day.

The years have gone by and time has passed
And still she remains my friend;
Her concerns about her sisters last,
And her love for us never ends.

And so on this day, I'm asking our Lord
That our sister He will bless
For all the wonderful things she's done,
For being a wonderful person to us.

Written for my sister, Susan L. Lloyd for her
birthday, May 20, 1998
~*Patricia A. Bayless Behnken*
July 5, 1998

Lovingly spoken,
She must be quite a special person..
She did a nice job if you are one of her
products..
I only had brothers and older boy cousins to
be there for me..
They were loving and caring and
supportive,
But your words suggest that I missed
something quite special,
In not having a "Susan " of my
own..
~Marilyn Souza

MY PRIZE FLOWER
Dedicated to Melinda Dague, Sarah Dague,
McCay Lloyd, and Bethany Mayberry

She picked a flower when she was small,
Then handed it to me;
As I saw her pick it from its place,
My heart cried with horror deep,
Oh no, my prize flower!
She's ruined it that's for sure!
But then I saw her smiling face,
With true happiness so pure,
Her little eyes danced with glee,
Her dimples showed so deep,
Her baby voice so tender spoke,
"A flower for you to keep!"
My heart warmed within me,
As she kissed me upon the cheek,
Her lips were soft as petals,
And I became so weak,
The flower became more valuable
Than it could ever be
Had it but stayed upon its stem
For all the world to see.

~*Patricia A. Bayless Behnken*
Oct. 18, 1997

OUR BABY BOY

Dedicated to Brian Dague, Phillip Dague,
Thomas Dague, Jack Dague, Spencer Lloyd,
and Adam Hultberg

Our little baby boy, so tender and sweet,
Our bundle of joy without any teeth!
Today you're so cuddly, so soft and smooth,
What will you look like with your first little tooth?

What do you think in your tiny little brain?
Are you dreaming of puppies or baseball or trains?
Or do you dream of Mommy's tender, sweet hug?
Or of Daddy's big smile as you lay on the rug?

What will you say when you speak your first word?
Will it be Mommy or Daddy or something else you heard?
How much we wonder as we look on your face,
And smooth back your hair and fluff your bed into place;

Eager and anxious to see you grow,
So that answers to our questions we will finally know;
Yet looking at you so precious, until
We find ourselves wishing that time would stand still.

~*Patricia A. Behnken*
September, 1993

THANK YOU
~Matthew 25:40

I searched my heart and could not find
A perfect gift for thee~
To one who's shown such love as you
In giving help to me.
So I decided to write a poem
To tell what's in my heart;
My thanks to you, much gratitude
To you I do impart.
My Lord is watching over me~
He's watching over thee;
With smiling eyes He knows these acts
And approves of what He sees.
He says if we believe in Him,
By faith He'll save our soul;
If we but give our life to Him,
He'll cleanse and make us whole.
But only faith is dead He says,
If works we do not do,
We must accept His sacrifice
Then tell others of Him too.
I have accepted Christ as King~
I am a child of God;
When helping me as you have done,
You are ministering to God.
He says if you have given help
To those in time of need,
As ye have done it unto the least of these,
Ye have done it unto Me.

Written for and dedicated to
Jeanette Haines
~*Patricia A. Bayless Behnken*

MY SISTER IN THE LORD
Dedicated to Marcie Carter
My prayer partner

My friend you are so special,
You mean so much to me,
My heart becomes so happy
when I see you smile at me;

Your face is all aglow,
Jesus' love you do reflect,
and so my special friend
you've gained my high respect.

I know that if I need you,
you'll be willing to be near
to help in ways you can
and fill my day with cheer.

So many times you've prayed
for things I was going through,
and times we prayed together
and you let me pray with you.

The early morning blessings
you helped to bring my way,
Our early morning prayers
helped start our happy day!

We both shared our hearts needs
when others were still in bed,
I knew you'd be faithful
And pray for all you said.

To me you'll always be special,
I'll always love you true;
And it feels so very special,
'cause I know you love me too!!!

~*Patricia A. Behnken*
August 2, 1998

SANDRA
Dedicated to Sandra Sherwood

Dear Sandra, our friendship to me is so dear,
I'm thankful God sent you to us for two
 years;
You are so special and are treasured so much
We feel God has blessed us with His special
 touch.

Along life's journey, I know that God is with
 you,
He leads you and guides you in whatever you
 do;
So, though it's hard for us to say good-bye,
We can do so in peace, though with a sigh.

I have been truly, personally blessed,
The joy in our friendship has been of the
 best;
I'm so thankful to God that you came our
 way
And brought sunshine and smiles to brighten
 our day.

No one can ever be like you in my heart,
For you are truly an original work of art,
With your soft-spoken ways and gentleness
And you love for the Lord that you always
 confess.

So, now as you go, we wish you the best:
We wish you joy, love and peace and all of
 the rest;
That you'll always feel the presence of God,
 we trust,
And we ask that your heart keeps a small
 place for us.

~Patricia A. Behnken
June 1, 1995

TAYVONA A SWEET TREAT

Cookie, you are really so sweet,
And knowing you is really a treat!
Your smiles can melt the hardest ice,
And hearing you laugh is really nice.

Your dimples usually always show,
The fact that you're happy is easy to know;
You're a person who is always so caring,
The joy you have you're always sharing.

Your artistic ability is really quite good,
To draw anything, maybe you could!
You can write, play drums, and even sing,
And pleasure through all these things you
   bring.

You are the sweetest Cookie, it's true,
And I sure am blessed by knowing you;
As the old saying goes, by others told,
"When God made you, He broke the mold!"

Dedicated with love in Christ
To Tayvona Moore (older
sister of Keith Booker)

~Patricia A. Behnken

CUPID DOVE

You go out of your way to spread
happiness and love,
and for this, to me you're a "Cupid Dove."

So many ways you have shown you care,
with your arrows of compassion twirling
through the air...

You aim to land a needy soul,
and with God's guidance it finds the goal.

I'm sure in God's eyes you do more than
  required,
For it's that "Cupid dove" in you
that never gets tired.

Then a life such as mine is so sweetly
touched and uplifted,
You are to me truly gifted.

Because of your quest to express
  true love,
I will never forget you, "Cupid Dove.

~Regina Moore
April, 1995

Sis. Pat....For all the thoughtful things
you've done, words cannot be
found to express my thanks to you.
   You have truly been a friend to me,
for it's the love of God in you I see.
   With a deep desire to do more that
you can, and a spirit so free to lend
  a hand.
You are so special to me.........

Regina

HEAVENLY

✝

PROMISES

TO FOLLOW

What do you mean when you say follow?
do you mean staying close behind?
Do you mean we're to keep our eyes straight on
and to keep from straying our mind?

Do you mean walking close and within His touch,
that His every move we see...
so the hem of His garment is within reach
and his virtue available to me?

Or do you mean to lag behind
and taking our good old time,
as long as we know He is somewhere ahead
and the choices of the path are mine?

So sights along the way that entice
will lure us to forsake the path,
that snares may start to encumber our way,
threatening with the enemy's wrath?

Though springs of water and mountains allure
with their beauty all divine,
I choose the following of Jesus close
so that His blessings will all be mine.

He'll speak to me as I speak to Him
He'll comfort me all through the day,
And when it's time to close my eyes in sleep,
to Heaven He will show me the way.

He won't just point the way and say go,
He'll hold my hand in His, so sweet,
and He will take me to Heaven with Him,
and together we'll walk golden streets.

~*Patricia A. Behnken*
Aug 2, 1998

Rev 21:1 *And I saw a new heaven and a new earth: for the first heaven and the first earth were passed away; and there was no more sea.*
Rev 21:2 *And I John saw the holy city, new Jerusalem, coming down from God out of heaven, prepared as a bride adorned for her husband.*
Rev 21:3 *And I heard a great voice out of heaven saying, Behold, the tabernacle of God is with men, and he will dwell with them, and they shall be his people, and God himself shall be with them, and be their God.*
Rev 21:4 *And God shall wipe away all tears from their eyes; and there shall be no more death, neither sorrow, nor crying, neither shall there be any more pain: for the former things are passed away.*

Rev 22:1 *And he shewed me a pure river of water of life, clear as crystal, proceeding out of the throne of God and of the Lamb.*
Rev 22:2 *In the midst of the street of it, and on either side of the river, was there the tree of life, which bare twelve manner of fruits, and yielded her fruit every month: and the leaves of the tree were for the healing of the nations.*
Rev 22:3 *And there shall be no more curse: but the throne of God and of the Lamb shall be in it; and his servants shall serve him:*
Rev 22:4 *And they shall see his face; and his name shall be in their foreheads.*
Rev 22:5 *And there shall be no night there; and they need no candle, neither light of the sun; for the Lord God giveth them light: and they shall reign for ever and ever.*

Rev 22:12 *And, behold, I come quickly; and my reward is with me, to give every man according as his work shall be.*
Rev 22:13 *I am Alpha and Omega, the beginning and the end, the first and the last.*

Rev 22:20 *He which testifieth these things saith, Surely I come quickly. Amen. Even so, come, Lord Jesus.*
Rev 22:21 *The grace of our Lord Jesus Christ be with you all. Amen.*

ABOUT THE POETS

PATRICIA A. BAYLESS BEHNKEN, from Ohio. . .
author/publisher...summary on back of book

NANCY BLYTHE, from Dayton, Ohio...
niece of Betty Barnett, also of Dayton, Ohio. Nancy passed away March 26, 1998 at age 44. She had three daughters, one son and one grandson. Her poem was lovingly written for her aunt, who was a great Godly influence in her life. Betty has much hope of seeing Nancy again one day in Heaven.

MARGARET BURCHFIELD, from Dayton, Ohio (home of Wilbur and Orville Wright and Paul Laurence Dunbar. Ohio is also the birthplace of Roy Rogers.)...
Margaret has lived in Dayton for many years, but is originally from North Carolina, the state of the Wright Brothers' first flight. She is married to Keenis Burchfield and has one daughter and four sons. She also raised a niece and a nephew in her home. She has ten grandchildren plus three. Margaret has worked with children in Sunday School and has nursing home ministries plus a variety of other Christian involvements.

KRISTI BUTLER, from Kentucky. . .
is married to James and has two children, Brittany, 7 and Austin, 6. She enjoys various crafts, being outside and writing poetry as inspired. She is admittedly a "laid back and relaxed" type individual, who believes that no child's question is unimportant, and that every day is special.

DORIS ALLEN DAVIS, from North Carolina ...
is married, and her husband's name is Steve. They have one daughter, Wendi, and two cats, Dolly and Tilly (can't forget the cats...they're in charge!). Doris is an active member of a small Baptist church, where she serves as church clerk/secretary, Sunday School teacher and Women's Missionary Union leader.

MEAGAN DOLIBER, from Massachusetts...
is a 15 year old freshman in high school. One poem she wrote was written when she was in a very difficult period in her life. She realized though, and says, "There is always Someone who loves me, even when I won't let myself be loved. Thanks for reading my poetry."

RICHARD L. ELAM, from Texas...
loves to write poetry when he is not reading history. Richard is a community college instructor in Texas. He is also an active member of a Baptist church serving as Deacon, Sunday School teacher, and member of the church orchestra. He and his wife, Pam have two sons.

JACK ELLIS, from Florida...
Senior citizen, employed full time visiting churches, and better yet getting to know members, their memories, their hopes, by listening to stories of their journey. Jack's wife is Barbara.

DONNA M. GIVENS, from Tennessee...
is mother of three wonderful daughters. She has two terrific granddaughters and a brand new grandson. She loves to read and write poetry and short stories. Her main goal is to print her own books, not to sell, but to leave behind for her children and grandchildren. Donna's favorite poet is Helen Steiner Rice, as she loves the simplicity of her poetry. The things she values most in her friends are kindness and a sense of humor. She feels that if she can't find something nice to say about someone that she shouldn't say anything at all.

LINDSEY INGRAM, from Illinois...
is a 15 year old female with a passion for God. The letter she wrote is dedicated to a little girl in her church who only lived to be two days old. Lindsey says, "It was a hard thing to write, but God gave the strength to make it easier." She met Jesus on September 13, 1997, and has never been the same! He has given her many awesome gifts, one of them is poetry. Her greatest wish is to use poetry to glorify God and to spread his Good News! Lindsey has also been putting out a periodic bulletin called FAITH. In addition to giving it out, she also sends it to many people through email. She has been a real blessing to a lot of us, and we appreciate her very much.

GENE HOLLINGSWORTH, from Ohio. . .
is author of the "Ball Game" ☺ Kim says he's the world's best father!

DOROTHY MARIE JACKSON, from Texas. . .
is a 16 year old who has been writing poetry for almost a year...She mainly likes to write poetry about Christ. She finds joy in writing it, and watching it change others' lives. She wants to continue writing poetry for Christ, and also hopes to one day show others to God through singing.

GARY JENKINS, from Illinois. . .
has been married to his precious wife Betty for twenty-three years. He has six children and twelve grandchildren. Gary believes that "the servant" is a name God gave to him for writing. He says that as to whether his poetry is good or not depends on who reads it. He writes for others and feels that God gives him a chance to share. He has met and talked to a lot of people he normally wouldn't have, because of his poetry.
Gary Jenkins personal quote:
" I am thankful to God for lots of things in my life, but most of all for Jesus. Everything is so much brighter if you can see the Light Of The Son".

SUSAN L. LLOYD, from Dayton, Ohio...
is the sister of author/publisher Patricia A. Bayless Behnken. Susan has been married to Darrel for thirty-five years, and they have two sons, Curt and Jeff and two daughters-in-law, Kathy and Alicia. Susan has a grandson, Spencer Lloyd and a granddaughter, McCay Lloyd.

KELLEY LUNDBORG, from Illinois . . .
was born in Chicago where she lived until she was 9, then lived 6 years in different southern states. She then moved back to the Chicago suburbs where she's lived and worked since. She has two absolutely beautiful children, both in college now and she couldn't be more proud. Kelley truly believes that to love and educate your children in the finest ways you know is the most valuable gift you can give them.

RENEE M. MALONE, from Pennsylvania. . .
is daughter of Patricia A. Bayless Behnken, author/ publisher. She was born and raised in Dayton, Ohio. She attended Free Gospel Bible Institute and graduated in May, 1989. She and Michael P. Malone Jr. were married in Sept of 1989, and they have three children: Jessica-8, Joshua-7 and Bethany-4.

INEZ REGINA MOORE, from Ohio. . .
is an illustrator of the books "Heavenly Dreams" and "Pathways Of My Journey" by Patricia A. Bayless Behnken. Regina is mother of four children: two daughters Tayvona and Shannon, and two sons: Joshua and Keith (in whose memory the book "Heavenly Dreams" is dedicated.) She is an active member of The First Pentecostal Church of Murlin Heights in Dayton, Ohio and is employed full-time at an automobile factory. Regina enjoys artwork, sewing and spending quality time with her children.

ALBERT N. RENSHAW, from Ohio. . .
is married to Carol. He works at a nursing home in Troy, Ohio as a state tested Nurse's Aid. Al is a member of Grace United Methodist Church and is active in the choir. He writes for his personal enjoyment.

LISA M. SACKETT, from Dayton, Ohio. . .
was in the banking industry both commercial and private for seven years and then decided to stay home when she was expecting her second child. She is happily married to Chris, who is the cover illustrator of this book, "Heavenly Dreams." He is in the airforce and is stationed at Wright Patt AFB. They have two boys, Nathan-9 and Cody-3. The family are active members of Bethel Temple Assemblies of God. Lisa home schools Nathan, who is going into the fourth grade. She says her favorite verse, Isaiah 43:2, has helped her go through hard times...knowing that God would take her through all things. Renee Behnken Malone and she grew up together and Lisa says that the lifetime friendship they share is a treasure; and though Renee is an only child, they will always be sisters by heart. (Thank you, Pat...for God's gift of Renee to you...and to me).

LANA ST JOHN, from Virginia...
is niece by marriage of Patricia Behnken. She is 17 years old and a junior in high school. She loves to write poetry in her spare time, and plans to be fulfilling her career as a licensed cosmetologist. Lana has gone through a lot of hard times in the past, but has learned to get through her problems and move on, she says, "because I know there are greater things in the future."

TRACY TAMMARO, from Minnesota...
has been writing poetry since she was a teenager. She is a Nurse in Internal Medicine and Pulmonary Med and also is Infection Control Coordinator and Nurse Supervisor. She loves to write spiritual poetry and says, "God gives me the words to write." She is married with two daughters ages 13 and 9. She and her family belong to the Assembly of God church in Minnesota.

SUZANNE VANDERBECK, from Putnam Country, New York...
is married and has one son, Michael, who feels called to pastor. She is a housewife and is waiting on the Lord for an upcoming ministry that He has promised her. She has been ministering to people online for eighteen months and says she has seen many saved, healed and delivered for the Lord. Suze has been writing since she was a child and feels that in 1996 she was given a specific gift of writing poetry for the Lord. Despite many extreme hardships in her life, she feels very blessed of the Lord and her greatest desire is to serve Him and be able to help other people to be saved, healed and delivered through her writing.

INDEX OF POETRY BY AUTHOR

NAME AND TITLE OF POEM   **PAGE NO.**

BEHNKEN, PATRICIA A. (Poems listed at end after all other poetry)

BLYTHE, NANCY
Jesus Is Here For Aunt Betty	163

BURCHFIELD, MARGARET
Oh What A Journey	71
Regrets But With Hope	87
The Lily	128
The Valley	128
Trust	71

BUTLER, KRISTI
Carry Me	22

DAVIS, DORIS ALLEN
A Mother's Love	161
Beneath The Olive Tree	42
Chasing After The Wind	114
Every Time A Soul Is Saved	130
From God's Precious Hand	54
Hidden In Plain View	44
I Have Never Seen An Angel	45
In His Hands	21
Let Me Bring Your Message	131
No One To Care	140
Put Your Hand In His Hand	88
She Was Never Alone	158
The Little Church	149
The Shield Of Scarlet	60
The Winding River	118
There Are No Limits	35

DOLIBER, MEAGAN
Free Skies	65
Saved	32
Tears From Heaven	64

ELLIS, JACK
Joy In The Journey	16
Memories Of Mom	162
On Letting Go	117
Within His Light	16

ELAM, RICHARD L.
    Christian Politics   119
    Not Them   100
    Prayer For Peace (Of Mind)   66
    Problems In The Garden   98
    Sin Sick   98
    Real Treasure   24
    Resurrection   30
    Selflessness Vs. Selfishness   107
    So Who's Perfect   34
    Woman's Fault   120

GIVENS, DONNA M.
    A Mother's Love   167
    Circle Of Love   148
    Garden Of The Heart   25
    I Believe   90
    Look Beyond   91
    Times Of Twilight   69

HOLLINGSWORTH, GENE
    The Ball Game   165

INGRAM, LINDSEY
    Letter To Mommy And Daddy   86

JACKSON, DOROTHY MARIE
    Why   47

JENKINS, GARY (The Servant)
    A Parent's Prayer   168
    A Wondrous Story   36
    Brighter Skies   84
    Fears Aren't The Same   92
    For Our Sakes   169
    He's Not Hurting Anymore   147
        (Dedication to James Schneider)   146
    He's Tasted The Tears   61
    Is Tonight The Night   101
    Praise In The Night Too   17
    Positions Of The Heart   102
    Silvered Halos   142
    Sometimes The Answer's No   121
    Statement of a Servant   103
    The Race   80
    Twinkling Of An Eye   115

LLOYD, SUSAN
   Grandma   156

LUNDBORG, KELLEY
   If I Could   137
   Rain   28
   Searching   116

MALONE, RENEE M.
   I Know I Can   59

MOORE, INEZ REGINA
   Cupid Dove   178
   I Know I Love You   26

RENSHAW, ALBERT N
   Natural Love   52

SACKETT, LISA M.
   Now He's Gone   104
   Sitting At His Feet   23
   Take The Time   112
   The Presence   20

ST JOHN, LANA
   They Don't Know Me   138
   With Thanksgiving   49

TAMMARRO, TRACY
   A Child Lost   134
   A Friend   162
   Angels   39
   Eyes On God   115
   From Death To Life   94
   God's Creations   38
   His Gift   29
   His Presence   29
   Keep Walking   76
   Our Guide In Life   77
   Walking In The Unknown   70
   What Would You Say   99

VANDERBECK, SUZANNE
   More   33
   Somehow   46
   Tears In His Eyes   48
   That I Might Rest   28

PATRICIA A. BAYLESS BEHNKEN

A Joyful Morn	93
A Memorial To Our Brother Jack Pyle	153
Another Chance	51
Apple of Friendship (The)	154
Basket Of Gifts	152
Cargo	14
Cautions	122
Christian Love?	110
Closer To You	74
Daddy	164
Delicious	159
Distance	151
Fight Back	125
Forgiveness	144
Hand (The)	75
Heavenly Dreams	5
His Hand Extented	141
Hope	58
I Am That I Am, The Presence	40
I Will Comfort Thee	67
Jesus Loves You	79
Jesus You Know	78
Joy In The Morning	155
Just Sing A Little Song	19
Life's Pathways	7
Lighthouse (The)	6
Like-Kind Christian Friends	150
Little Voices	135
Mother	160
My Daughter My Friend	166
My First Parade	165
My Little Lamb	82
My Prize Flower	172
My Sister In The Lord (Marcie)	175
My Teacher, Grace Hart	145
Nothing To Do	132
On Death Row	72
Our Baby Boy	173
Pathways Of My Journey	56
Praise In The Night	17
Praise The Lord Anyhow!	18
Prayer Of A Teacher	136
Pursued	124
Rainbow (The)	10
Released	126
Resurrection (The)	43
Sandra	176

(Continued poetry by Patricia A. Bayless Behnken)

Soldiers Of Christ	133
Susan, My Sister, My Second Mother, My Teacher, My Friend	170
Tayvona, A Sweet Treat	177
Thank You	174
Thank You Lord	50
Thanksgiving	53
To Follow	180
To Write	14
Trials	63
True Love Vs. Emotions	109
What Is Joy?	108
What Is Man?	37
When You Don't Feel Like Singing	68
With Jesus Never Alone	62
Ye Are The Light	139

For comments or information regarding either "Heavenly Dreams" or "Pathways Of My Journey" by Patricia A. Bayless Behnken, write to or email the following addresses:

Patricia A. Bayless Behnken
Morning Joy Publishing Company
P. O. Box 702
Vandalia, OH 45377-0702

Email:
MornJoyPB@aol.com

Additional copies of "Heavenly Dreams" are normally $10.95 plus tax and/or shipping, if applicable. You may ask if a discount applies.